# Fur, Feathers, Scales, and Skin

## Teacher's Resource Module

Lynn Bryan

### CONSULTANTS

Ron Benson

Harold Fenlon

Ken MacInnis

Kim Newlove

Charolette Player

Annetta Probst

### GENERAL EDITOR

Kathleen Doyle

Prentice Hall Ginn Canada
Scarborough, Ontario

**Canadian Cataloguing in Publication Data**

Main entry under title:
Fur, feathers, scales, and skin. Teacher's resource module

(Collections)
ISBN 0-13-010343-8 Atlantic Edition
ISBN 0-13-010344-6 Ontario Edition
ISBN 0-13-010345-4 Western Edition

1. Reading (Elementary). 2. Animals - Study and teaching (Elementary). I.
Benson, Ron, 1942- .

PE1127.A6F872 1996   428.6   C96-930687-3

Copyright © 1999 Prentice Hall Ginn Canada,
Scarborough, Ontario
ALL RIGHTS RESERVED.

No part of this book may be reproduced in any form or
by any means without permission in writing from the
publishers. Pages marked with the copyright symbol © may
be reproduced by the purchasing school.

Prentice Hall Inc., Upper Saddle River, New Jersey
Prentice Hall International, Inc., London
Prentice Hall of Australia, Pty., Sydney
Prentice Hall of India Pvt., Ltd., New Delhi
Prentice Hall of Japan, Inc., Tokyo
Prentice Hall of Southeast Asia (PTE) Ltd., Singapore
Editora Prentice-Hall do Brasil Ltda., Rio de Janeiro
Prentice-Hall Hispanoamericana, S.A., Mexico

ISBN 0-13-010343-8 Atlantic Edition
ISBN 0-13-010344-6 Ontario Edition
ISBN 0-13-010345-4 Western Edition
*Publisher:* Kathleen Doyle
*Managing Editor:* Linda McGuire
*Editorial Services:* First Folio Resource Group
*Copy/Production Editor:* Debbie Davies
*Production Co-ordinator:* Stephanie Cox
*Permissions:* Angelika Baur
*Design:* Word & Image Design Studio Inc.
*Illustrations* pp. 12, 21, 27, 28, 84, BLMs 3 and 16: Vesna Krstanovich

Printed and bound in Canada by Best Book Manufacturers.
1 2 3 4 5 6 BBM 02 01 00 99 98 97

## CREDITS

BLM 4: "Cat" by Mary Britton Miller. Appeared in *An Arkful of Animals*,
selected by William Cole. Copyright © 1978 Houghton Mifflin.
BLM 7: Book jacket copy from *The Wounded Wolf*, copyright © 1978 by
Jean Craighead George. Reprinted with permission.
BLMs 11 & 12: "Killer whales make cellular calls!" Appeared in *In Touch*.
Published by BC TEL Mobility Cellular, Fall 1995.
BLM 13: "Musk Oxen" by Igjugarjuk. Appeared in *Songs Are Thoughts:
Poems of the Inuit*, selected by Neil Philip. Copyright © 1995 Doubleday
Canada Limited.
BLM 18: "The Accident." Published by B.M.P. from *Baseball, Snakes, and
Summer Squash* by Donald Graves, 1996.
Covers pp. 1, 4, 92, 93, 96, 99, 102: *Gaddy's Story* reproduced with
permission of Breakwater Books Ltd. *Dragon in the Rocks* by permission
of Owl Books, Canada. *Lost and Found* reprinted by permission of
Penguin Books Canada Limited. Cover design: Pronk & Associates.
Cover illustration: Leung O'Young. *Pelly* by permission of Coteau Books.
Cover illustration and design by Bill Johnson.

## Sources for resources on page 5
*Links to Media*
- The Children's Group, 1400 Bayly Street, Suite 7, Pickering, ON
  L1W 3R2 Toll-free: 1-800-668-0242
- McIntyre Media Ltd., 30 Kelfield Street, Rexdale, ON  M9W 5A2
  Tel: 905-678-9866
- National Film Board. Toll-free: Atlantic Canada: 1-800-561-7104;
  Quebec: 1-800-363-0328; Ontario: 1-800-267-7710; Western and
  Northern Canada: 1-800-661-9867
- School Services of Canada, 66 Portland Street, Toronto, ON
  M5V 2M8 Toll-free: 1-800-387-2084
- T.H.A. Media Distributors Ltd., 1200 W. Pender Street, #307,
  Vancouver, BC  V6E 2S9 Toll-free: 1-800-661-4919

*Links to the Information Highway*
- Broderbund Software, P.O. Box 6125, Novato, CA  94948-6125 Toll-
  free: 1-800-521-6263; Educational support line: 1-800-474-8840
  Distribute: *The Print Shop Deluxe*
- The Children's Software Company, 5505 Connecticut Avenue N.W.,
  Suite #333, Washington, DC  20015-2601 Toll-free: 1-800-556-5590;
  Fax: 1-703-759-9402
  Distribute: *3-D Dinosaur Adventure, Davidson's Zoo Keeper, In the
  Company of Whales*
- Core Curriculum Technologies/Software Plus, #1-12760 Bathgate Way,
  Richmond, BC, V6V 1Z4 Toll-free: 1-800-663-7731; Fax: 604-273-6534
  Distribute: *In the Company of Whales, Super Paint 3.5 Deluxe*
- Educational Resources, 38 Scott Street West, St. Catharines, ON
  L2R 1C9 Toll-free: 1-800-565-5198; Ontario: 905-988-3577;
  Fax: 1-800-311-4600
  Distribute: *3-D Dinosaur Adventure, In the Company of Whales, Life in the
  Desert, Mammals: A Multimedia Encyclopedia CD, The Print Shop Deluxe,
  Super Paint 3.5 Deluxe*
- Educator's Choice Software Company, 29 Meadowview Drive,
  Bedford, NS  B4A 2C3 Tel: 902-452-6313; Fax: 902-832-0167
  Distribute: *3-D Dinosaur Adventure, Super Paint 3.5 Deluxe*

## ACKNOWLEDEGMENTS

Prentice Hall Ginn Canada wishes to express its sincere appreciation to
the following Canadian educators for contributing their time and
expertise during the development of this teacher's resource module.

Kathryn D'Angelo, Vice-Principal, Tomsett Elementary School, Richmond,
BC

Lorraine Prokopchuk, Language Arts Coordinator, St. James-Assiniboia
School Division #2, Winnipeg, MB

Lori Rog, Language Arts Consultant, Regina Public Schools, Regina, SK

Fred Schriver, Teacher, Centennial Elementary, Woodstock, NB

Sandra Sutton, Teacher, St. Richard School, Mississauga, ON

Marie Wiseman, Program Coordinator, Appalachia Roman Catholic
School Board, Stephenville, NF

**Literature Suggestions**, page 5:
Margaret Mackey, University of Alberta, AB

**Link to the Information Highway**, page 5:
Debbie Miller, Teacher, École Van Walleghem School, Winnipeg, MB

Prentice Hall Ginn Canada would also like to express its appreciation to
the staff and students of Warden Avenue Junior Public School,
Scarborough, Ontario, and of Malmo Elementary, Edmonton, Alberta, for
their assistance with this publication.

ii   *Collections 4*

# Contents

| ABOUT THE UNIT | 2 |
|---|---|

## TEACHING PLANS FOR SELECTIONS IN FUR, FEATHERS, SCALES, AND SKIN ANTHOLOGY ... 10

- Animal Profiles .................................................. 10
- Desert Tortoise .................................................. 17
- Lily Pad Pond .................................................... 23
- The Wounded Wolf ............................................ 30
- student writing .................................................. 36
- From a Whale-Watcher's Diary ............................ 37
- Animal Crimes, Animal Clues .............................. 43
- The Northern Way .............................................. 50
- student writing .................................................. 56
- The Puff Adder Who Was Stuck .......................... 57
- Digging Up Dinosaurs ........................................ 62
- An Interview with Father Goose .......................... 68
- student writing .................................................. 73
- You Asked About Pets ........................................ 74
- Keeping Old Friends .......................................... 79
- Pet Poems ........................................................ 85
- student writing .................................................. 91

## TEACHING PLANS FOR GENRE BOOKS AND NOVELS ... 92

- Gaddy's Story .................................................... 93
- Dragon in the Rocks .......................................... 96
- Lost and Found .................................................. 99
- Pelly ................................................................ 102

## ASSESS THE UNIT ... 106

## BLACKLINE MASTERS ... 109

## APPENDICES ... 137

- Appendix 1: Index to Key Learning Outcomes/Expectations ..... 138
- Appendix 2: Teaching Plans at a Glance ........................ 140
- Appendix 3: Unit Spelling Words ................................ 142

# About the Unit

The selections and learning opportunities in this inquiry unit focus on the relationships between people and animals, in the home and in the wild.

## Unit Focus

This unit will help students to develop concepts pertaining to
- **animals in different habitats**, including deserts, ponds, and the far north.
- **relationships and interactions** between people and animals, including how people study and protect animals.
- **people and pets**, including information about common household pets.

Throughout the unit, students will have many opportunities to
- make connections between the relationships presented in the literature in *Fur, Feathers, Scales, and Skin* and the relationships they have with animals in the world around them.
- use language for many purposes, most notably to
  – gather and organize information.
  – report and document factual information in different ways.
  – question and investigate topics, issues, and information pertaining to animals.
  – inform others about animals.
  – persuade/convince others of a point of view.
  – examine features of various forms of non-fiction text, including news articles, diary entries, interviews, personal essays, and question and answer formats.

2  Collections 4

# Language Arts Learning Expectations

As students participate in the learning experiences in the *Fur, Feathers, Scales, and Skin* unit, they will meet expectations pertaining to the following:

### Reading

Students will
- identify various forms of writing and describe their main characteristics—profiles, poems, photo essays, picture book stories, short stories, diary entries, news articles, interviews, questions and answers
- read a variety of fiction and non-fiction materials for different purposes
- state their own interpretation of a written work, using evidence from the work and from their own knowledge and experience
- identify the main idea in a piece of writing, and provide supporting details
- make inferences while reading
- develop their opinions by reading a variety of materials

### Writing

Students will
- communicate ideas and information for a variety of purposes and to specific audiences—newspaper articles, business letters, profiles, observation records, poems
- organize and develop ideas using paragraphs
- begin to write for more complex purposes
- produce pieces of writing using a variety of specific forms
- choose words that are most effective for their purposes

### Oral Communication

Students will
- express and respond to ideas and opinions concisely and clearly
- demonstrate the ability to concentrate by identifying main points and staying on topic
- communicate a main idea about a topic and describe a short sequence of events
- express and respond to ideas and opinions concisely and clearly
- use appropriate tone of voice and gestures in social and classroom activities

### Visual Communication

Students will
- create media works—diagrams, borders, mimes
- analyze media works—photographs, diagrams, illustrations, borders

(See *Appendix 1* for specific indicators of each expectation.)

# UNIT RESOURCES

## Student Books

### ANTHOLOGY

The *Fur, Feathers, Scales, and Skin* **anthology** contains a range of non-fiction and fiction selections of both published and student writing. It is intended for instructional use in a whole class or group teaching/learning context.

### GENRE BOOKS AND NOVELS

There are two **genre books** and two **novels** to provide sustained reading of longer prose pieces. They can be used in small group literature circles for book and novel study.

### Genre Books

- *Gaddy's Story: The First Weeks in the Life of an Atlantic Cod* by Sally V. Goddard. Through first-person narration and photographs of magnifications, an Atlantic cod tells about its first few weeks of life.

- *Dragon in the Rocks* by Marie Day. This biography, based on the childhood of Mary Anning, describes the young paleontologist's discovery of important dinosaur fossils in the cliffs around Lyme Regis, England.

### Novels

- *Lost and Found* by Jean Little. Lucy makes her first friend in a new town—a stray dog named Trouble. But when her parents and the girl down the street begin to look for Trouble's owner, Lucy realizes that she may lose her new friend.

- *Pelly* by Dave Glaze. When Sandra moves to Saskatoon with her father, she forms a special friendship with a wild pelican she feeds on the river. When the bird doesn't migrate, she must struggle to feed and protect it through the cold prairie winter.

Strategies for using the genre books and novels can be found on pages 92–105 of this guide and in the book *Teaching with Novels, Books, and Poetry*.

## Teacher Materials

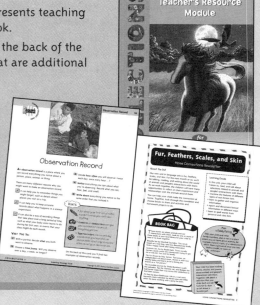

The **Teacher's Resource Module** for *Fur, Feathers, Scales, and Skin* presents teaching and assessment activities for each of the selections in the student book.

The **blackline masters** intended for use with this unit are included at the back of the Teacher's Resource Module. The blackline masters include masters that are additional activities and home link masters.

*Learning Strategy Cards* used in this thematic unit are:

28. Skim and Post-It
29. Learning Log
30. Observation Record
31. Writing a Paragraph
32. Report
33. Book Review
34. Newspaper Article
35. Using the Internet
36. Business Letter
37. Interviewing
38. Concrete and Shape Poetry

These cards are available within the COLLECTIONS 4 *Teacher's Resources* as a pack of 62 cards. Templates for some cards are available on disk (compatible with Mac and IBM).

4 Collections 4

## Read-Aloud Books

Choose a book to read aloud throughout this unit.
- Herriot, James. *James Herriot's Cat Stories*. Toronto: McClelland & Stewart, 1994. 156 pp.
- McKeever, Katherine. *Granny's Gang*. Toronto: Greey de Pencier, 1984. 95 pp. Note: True story about the author's owl rehabilitation centre.
- Mowat, Farley. *The Dog Who Wouldn't Be*. Toronto: McClelland & Stewart, 1992 © 1957. 238 pp.
- Naylor, Phyllis Reynolds. *Shiloh*. New York: Dell, 1991. 144 pp. Note: Protagonist has a .22 rifle.
- Sewell, Anna. *Black Beauty*. Richmond Hill, ON: Scholastic Canada, 1993. 168 pp.

## Personal Reading

With help from the school librarian and the students, assemble a classroom library of books pertaining to animals for students to browse through and choose for personal reading. The following books are suggested:
- Aska, Warabé. *Aska's Sea Creatures*. Poetry by David Day. Toronto: Doubleday, 1994. 32 pp.
- Cameron, Anne. *The Gumboot Geese*. Madeira Park, BC: Harbour, 1992. 40 pp.
- Citra, Becky. *My Homework Is in the Mail!* Richmond Hill, ON: Scholastic, 1995. 82 pp.
- Funston, Sylvia. *The Dinosaur Question and Answer Book*. Toronto: Greey de Pencier, 1992. 64 pp.
- Godkin, Celia. *Wolf Island*. Markham, ON: Fitzhenry & Whiteside, 1993. 36 pp.
- Greenland, Caroline. *Chimpanzees*. Markham, ON: Grolier, 1990. 48 pp.
- Hutchins, Pat. *Rats!* New York: Greenwillow, 1989. 96 pp.
- Kalman, Bobbie. *Arctic Animals*. Toronto/New York: Crabtree, 1988. 57 pp.
- Lucas, Zoe. *Wild Horses of Sable Island*. Toronto: Greey de Pencier, 1981. 34 pp.
- Manson, Ainslie. *A Dog Came, Too*. Toronto: Groundwood, 1992.
- Miles, Victoria. *Bald Eaglets*. Victoria: Orca, 1995. Unpaginated.
- Morton, Alexandra. *Siwiti — A Whale's Story*. Victoria: Orca, 1991. 49 pp.
- Sneyd, Lola. *Classy Cats*. Toronto: Simon & Pierre, 1991. 69 pp.
- Stolz, Mary. *Cat Walk*. New York: Harper Trophy, 1983. 120 pp. Note: Boy mistreats a cat.
- Swanson, Diane. *Why Seals Blow Their Noses*. Vancouver: Whitecap Books, 1992. 70 pp.
- Thornhill, Jan. *Wild in the City*. Toronto: Owl Books, 1995. Unpaginated.
- Wilson, Budge. *Harold and Harold*. Lawrencetown Beach, Nova Scotia: Pottersfield Press, 1995.

## Links to Media

These videos relate to topics dealt with in the unit.
- *Born to Be Wild: Funny, Furry, Fuzzy, Fun! (Owl TV)*. The Children's Group, 1994. 30 min.
- *The Boy and the Snowgoose*. National Film Board, 1984. 11 min.
- *Messages in Stone*. T.H.A. Media Distributors, 1993. 52 min.
- *Paws, Claws, Feathers & Fins: A Kid's Guide to Pets*. McIntyre Media, 1993. 30 min.
- *Storyteller: Michael Arvaarluk Kusugak*. School Services of Canada, 1995. 19 min.

## Links to the Information Highway

Software such as that listed below can be used to extend learning on the topic or on selected learning outcomes of the unit.
- *3-D Dinosaur Adventure* from Knowledge Adventure: As students travel back in time, they learn about dinosaurs and the age in which they lived. *IBM disk and CD-ROM; Mac CD-ROM*
- *Davidson's Zoo Keeper* from Davidson & Associates: In this problem solving program, students act as apprentice zoo-keepers who learn fascinating facts about animal habits and needs as part of their work. *IBM/Mac disk*
- *In the Company of Whales* from Discovery Channel: Students learn about the mysteries of whales through video footage, still images, graphics, and interviews with whale experts. *MPC CD-ROM*
- *Life in the Desert* from REmedia: This software includes information about desert regions and the plant and animal species that live there. *Mac/MPC CD-ROM*
- *Mammals: A Multimedia Encyclopedia CD* from National Geographic: Video clips, sound, photographs, fact boxes, and range maps provide information on more than 200 animals.
- *The Print Shop Deluxe* from Broderbund: 300 graphics and 30 fonts allow students to create banners, posters, bookmarks, and many other print formats. *IBM/Mac/Win 3.5 disk*
- *Super Paint 3.5 Deluxe* from Adobe: Students can use this graphics program to experiment with brightness, contrast, textures, and other elements of painting or drawing. *Mac CD-ROM*

Note: Sources for these videos and software products are listed with the credits on page (ii).

*About the Unit*  5

# UNIT OVERVIEW

| Topic Focus | FUR, FEATHERS, SCALES, AND SKIN Anthology ◆ = Canadian 🎧 = available on audio (student writing is indented) | Genre | Reading Level Range 2 3 4 5 | COLLECTIONS 4 Genre Book Links |
|---|---|---|---|---|
| **ANIMALS IN THE WILD** | ◆ Animal Profiles | profiles | 4 | ◆ *Gaddy's Story* by Sally V. Goddard  2 3 4 5 |
|  | Desert Tortoise | poem | |  |
|  | Lily Pad Pond | photo essay | 4 |  |
|  | 🎧 The Wounded Wolf | picture book story | 5 |  |
|  | 🎧 ◆ Wetlands Essay | essay | |  |
|  | 🎧 ◆ Ker-loo, Ker-lee-oo | factual narrative | |  |
|  | 🎧 ◆ Sea Otter | poem | |  |
| **PEOPLE'S INTERACTIONS WITH WILD ANIMALS** | 🎧 ◆ From a Whale-Watcher's Diary | diary entries | 5 | ◆ *Dragon in the Rocks* by Marie Day  2 3 4 5 |
|  | Animal Crimes, Animal Clues | article | 5 |  |
|  | 🎧 ◆ The Northern Way | personal essay | 4 |  |
|  | ◆ Ernest Thompson Seton | biography | |  |
|  | ◆ Mary Gauthier | essay | |  |
|  | Naomi's Geese | book review | |  |
|  | ◆ The Puff Adder Who Was Stuck | picture book story | 4 |  |
|  | ◆ Digging Up Dinosaurs | news articles | 5 |  |
|  | 🎧 ◆ An Interview with Father Goose | interview | 4 |  |
|  | ◆ Letters from Endangered Animals | letters | |  |
|  | ◆ Piping Plover | memoir | |  |
| **PEOPLE AND PETS** | ◆ You Asked About Pets | questions & answers | 4 |  |
|  | 🎧 Keeping Old Friends | short story | 5 |  |
|  | Pet Poems | poems | |  |
|  | ◆ Special Jobs, Special People | personal narrative | |  |
|  | ◆ Horses | poem | |  |
|  | Rescue K-9-1 | personal narrative | |  |

## Criteria for Reading Level Range

**Key:** The Reading Level Range is the independent level. The solid boxes indicate the overall readability. The dot indicates the range.
**Note:** For some students, introductory work with the topic-specific and/or technical vocabulary may be needed.

### Factors that we considered:
- **concept load:** number and nature of new concepts, amount of exemplification, contextual support
- **language considerations:** vocabulary, sentence patterns, and complexity
- **writing style and tone:** familiar or unfamiliar, informal or formal
- **genre type and structure:** familiarity, predictability, and repetitiveness of the elements of the story or writing form
- **selection length**
- **classroom reality:** selections represent a range of abilities in a Grade 4 classroom

### Factors that you may also consider:
- **familiarity:** each student's background knowledge and familiarity with the topic
- **student interest:** each student's degree of interest in and motivation for the topic and/or content of the selection
- **reading stage/level of the student:** whether he/she can read it independently,

6  Collections 4

| COLLECTIONS 4 Novel Links | Other COLLECTIONS 4 Anthology Links | Other PRENTICE HALL GINN Links |
|---|---|---|
| | The Buzz of a Bee (Unit 4) *poem*<br>Dancing Bees (Unit 4) *article*<br>Fireflies (Unit 4) *poem* | In Search of the Great Bears (L10)<br>It's a Frog's Life (L10)<br>Monsters of Deep (SUN7)<br>Secrets of the Desert (L9)<br>The Song of the Mantis (L9)<br>Spider Relatives (L10) |
| ❦<br>*Pelly*<br>by Dave Glaze<br><br>2  3  4  5 | The Biggest Scare (Unit 2) *true tale*<br>The Day Grandfather Tickled a Tiger (Unit 2) *true tale*<br>Fly Away Home (Unit 1) *picture book story*<br>Fox Song (Unit 1) *picture book story*<br>A Wild Bear and Her Cubs (Unit 2) *poem* | Dinosaur Bones (SUN8)<br>Fernitickles (L10)<br>Helping the Hoiho (L9)<br>Old Jasper (SUN8)<br>Shark Rescue (SUN7)<br>Snake! (SUN2)<br>Wing High, Gooftah (L10) |
| ❦<br>*Lost and Found*<br>by Jean Little<br><br>2  3  4  5 | I Wish I Were the Oldest (Unit 1) *short story* | A Pony for Penny (SUN10)<br>Best Dog in the Whole World (SUN6)<br>Best Friends (TS)<br>The Foundling (TS)<br>Old Bones (SUN5)<br>Shambles (SUN10)<br>Too Busy for Pets! (SUN3) |

**Keys:**

The COLLECTIONS 4 units referred to in the second last column are as follows:
Unit 1: *Within My Circle*
Unit 2: *Tales—Tall, True, Old, and New*
Unit 4: *And the Message Is...*
Unit 5: *Building Community*

Letter codes in the last column indicate the following Prentice Hall Ginn publications:
S4 = *Journeys: Springboards 4*
TS = *Journeys: Tickle the Sun*

L9 = *Literacy 2000: Stage 9*
L10 = *Literacy 2000: Stage 10*
SUN2 = *Sunshine Books: Level 2*
SUN3 = *Sunshine Books: Level 3*
SUN4 = *Sunshine Books: Level 4*
SUN5 = *Sunshine Books: Level 5*
SUN6 = *Sunshine Books: Level 6*
SUN7 = *Sunshine Books: Level 7*
SUN8 = *Sunshine Books: Level 8*
SUN9 = *Sunshine Books: Level 9*
SUN10 = *Sunshine Books: Level 10*
SUN11 = *Sunshine Books: Level 11*

with teacher guidance, with peer support, or in a listen-and-read approach only
• *reading strategy used*: the reading strategies suggested in the *Teacher's Resource Module* are intended to allow most Grade 4 students to enjoy and understand the selections
• *language level of the student*: whether or not the student's birth language is English

*About the Unit*    7

# ONGOING LEARNING OPPORTUNITIES

The following activities can be initiated over two to three days to

- launch student interest in the unit.
- provide a common base for class, group, or individual learning experiences.
- engage students in sustained learning throughout the unit.
- establish a procedure for spelling workshops.

## Read aloud a book

Choose one or more of the books on page 5 to read aloud to the class throughout the unit study.

## Establish a writing area

Create an environment that supports process writing. Explain to the students that they can use this area to write about topics they are interested in, to discuss their writing with you or one another, to consult reference sources, and to keep their writing portfolios.

Involve the students in preparing the writing area by suggesting that they begin a chart of various ways to present factual information. The student writing pages in *Fur, Feathers, Scales, and Skin* contain ideas and models. The students can continue to build their chart as they encounter new ideas in this unit or develop their own ideas.

## Set up an inquiry area

Establish an area where the students can pursue their inquiries about animals. Include resources such as fiction and non-fiction books, magazines, pictures, photographs, atlases, and dictionaries; items from the natural environment; and concrete materials such as models. Encourage students to bring in materials for the area and to help arrange the space.

Include display space for the students' writing and investigations so that students have opportunities to learn from each other. They might add their animal reports, charts, and other print and non-print work, such as tapes and computer disks, to the area. Students could also use this space to post "want ads" asking for partners interested in pursuing the same topics, or requesting resources to use in their inquiries.

## Organize an audiovisual/ technology library

Set aside an area as an audiovisual/technology library. Invite the students to choose from a variety of materials appropriate to their abilities and needs. They can watch videos, films, and filmstrips of animals; listen to recordings of animal sounds; explore CD-ROMs and videodiscs that focus on animals in different regions; and experiment with software related to animals. Using the computer, they could write and illustrate in a variety of modes and styles— newspaper articles, illustrated glossaries, poems, profiles—then display their writing or share it with classmates, friends, or family members.

Look for this symbol throughout the unit to find links to computers, other electronic media, and technical writing.

## Link to the home

To reinforce learning between the home and the school,
- use the *Home Connections Newsletter*, Blackline Masters 1–2. Send these pages home throughout the unit, as appropriate.
- encourage students to bring from home books, magazines, video cassettes, computer games, or other media pertaining to animals. They can share these with classmates or include them in the classroom inquiry area or audiovisual/technology library.
- encourage students to share with siblings and other family members favorite articles, stories, or poems they have read or written throughout the unit.
- look for the home link symbol 🏠 throughout the unit.

## Plan for spelling workshops

Spelling strategies and activities are provided in the teaching plans throughout the *Fur, Feathers, Scales, and Skin* unit. In this unit and in subsequent units of COLLECTIONS, the focus is to integrate spelling with reading and writing.

Teachers can
- choose a few **high utility words** to focus on each week, perhaps in collaboration with the students. Refer to high utility lists compiled by people such as Ves Thomas, Mary Tarasoff, Rebecca Sitton, or Edward Fry.
- have students select some **personal words** they would like to learn to spell. They can draw these words from various subject areas, from personal writing errors, from words related to the theme, or from other words that interest them. *Keeping a Personal Dictionary*, Learning Strategy Card 1, can be used to help students choose and keep a record of their words.
- use or adapt the **unit spelling words** compiled from the individual prose selections. These words highlight particular patterns and strategies. (See *Appendix 3*, page 142, for an overview of the unit spelling words.)
- use the **blackline masters** provided with each selection to produce word cards for sorting and study. (See *Language Workshop — Spelling*, page 16 of this guide.)

For each group of spelling words, there are specific activities in the *Language Workshop — Spelling* section of the selection teaching plan.

*About the Unit* 9

# Animal Profiles

These profiles of animals from different animal groups feature concise descriptions, fabulous facts, and close-up photographs.

Anthology, pages 4–11
Blackline Master 21
Learning Strategy Card 28

## Learning Choices

**LINK TO EXPERIENCE**

Think of Ways to Gather Information

Classify Animals

**READ AND RESPOND TO TEXT**

READING FOCUS
- state their own interpretation of a written work, using evidence from the work and from their own knowledge and experience
- STRATEGY: **read, paraphrase, and teach**

**REVISIT THE TEXT**

READING
Research an Animal
- read a variety of fiction and non-fiction materials for different purposes

WRITING
Write an Animal Profile
- produce pieces of writing using a variety of specific forms
Language Workshop — Spelling
- plurals: -s, -es, and -ies endings; irregular plurals

ORAL COMMUNICATION
Listen for Fabulous Facts
- demonstrate the ability to concentrate by identifying main points and staying on topic

**LINK TO CURRICULUM**

SCIENCE
Find Out About Food Chains

MATHEMATICS
Create and Solve Mathematics Problems

LANGUAGE ARTS
Write an Animal Adventure Story

Begin an Animal Word Bank

## Key Learning Expectations

Students will
- state their own interpretation of a written work, using evidence from the work and from their own knowledge and experience **(Reading Focus, p. 11)**
- read a variety of fiction and non-fiction materials for different purposes **(Reading Mini Lesson, p. 12)**
- produce pieces of writing using a variety of specific forms **(Writing Mini Lesson, p. 13)**
- demonstrate the ability to concentrate by identifying main points and staying on topic **(Oral Communication Mini Lesson, p. 13)**

## LINK TO EXPERIENCE

### Think of Ways to Gather Information

Ask the students to tell what they know about a specific animal and where they learned their information. List their facts and information sources in a chart. Together, evaluate the reliability of the sources, and suggest ways to verify and gain further information. Add new sources to the list for future reference.

| What I already know about sharks | Where I learned this |
|---|---|
| Sharks are dangerous. | from a movie |
| They live in warm-water oceans. | in a book on sharks |
| Sharks have very big, ragged teeth. | from a poster |
| Most baby sharks are born alive like humans. | on an encyclopedia CD-ROM |
| Don't swim at beaches where sharks are sighted. | from a friend, who read this in a travel brochure |

10 *Collections 4*

### Classify Animals

Write the names of the different animal groups on the board: birds, insects, mammals, fish, and reptiles. Have students brainstorm animals for each category, and invite them to give reasons for their classification. Through discussion, elicit that there are different ways to classify animals and that animals from different groups may share similar characteristics.

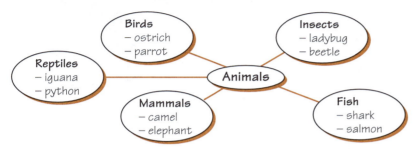

# READ AND RESPOND TO TEXT

### Reading Focus

Use a variation of the read and paraphrase strategy—**read, paraphrase, and teach**. Model the strategy by reading the "Monarch Butterfly" animal profile to the students. Together, discuss what the headings mean, and ask the students what information is new to them or is being confirmed. Then, invite volunteers to summarize orally, as if they were teaching someone, what they learned from the profile.

Students could use the *jigsaw co-operative learning strategy* to read the other profiles. They would form expert groups in which they read and discuss the animal profile for which they are responsible. Then, they would return to their "home" groups to teach and share what they learned. In this way, all students become "experts" on the animals.

### Reader Response

Students could
- gather fiction and non-fiction books about animals for an animal book display.
- make an animal poster that includes an illustration or photo and some interesting information. Students might design their poster using a graphics/text program such as *The Print Shop Deluxe*. (See pages 5 and (ii) for more information.)
- write a poem about an animal in the selection.
- create animal riddles using information from the profiles.
- tell a partner the most interesting fact that they learned.

### Get Ready to Read

Have the students scan the selection to determine that they will be reading about animals in five different categories. Elicit the type of information they think they will find as well as any information they might already know.

#### GENERAL JIGSAW STRATEGY

Students form "home" groups, where each group member is given a number. The "home" groups separate, and each member joins a new group formed by students with the same number. These groups become "experts" at an assigned task.

When the task is complete, members of "expert" groups return to their "home" groups. The students teach the other group members what they learned in their "expert" groups.

*Animal Profiles* 11

## ONGOING ASSESSMENT

Note:

- [ ] Are students able to locate pertinent information?
- [ ] Can they organize the information by heading?
- [ ] Do students use the Skim and Post-It strategy to research various topics?

# REVISIT THE TEXT

## Reading

### Research an Animal

*Learning Strategy Card 28*

Choose an animal that you and the students would like to find out more about, then list questions that you have about that animal. Using Learning Strategy Card 28, model how to use the Skim and Post-It strategy to gather and organize information.

Group related questions, assigning a different heading and number to each group. Skim through print resources and place self-stick notes beside information that seems to answer the questions. Write on the note the number code and any comments that might be useful.

| Questions | Heading | Number Code |
|---|---|---|
| Where do penguins live? | Range | 1 |
| What do they eat? | Food | 2 |
| What do penguins look like? | Description | 3 |
| Why can't they fly? | Description | 3 |
| What are the different kinds of penguins? | Species | 4 |
| Where do penguins lay their eggs? | Lifestyle | 5 |
| How do they care for their young? | Lifestyle | 5 |

3: Penguins haven't been able to fly for millions of years.

4: The largest penguins are the emperor penguins.

5: Penguins lay their eggs in huge colonies called rookeries.

To consolidate the information, have students read aloud, paraphrase, or show illustrations that answer each question. Then, summarize and record the answers under each heading. Ask the students how categorizing and coding information in this way helps them with their research.

Students could use the Skim and Post-It strategy to gather and record information for the other headings. Or, they could use this strategy to research the animal they chose for their personal inquiry.

12  Collections 4

## Writing

### Write an Animal Profile

Encourage the students to recall how the information in each animal profile is organized. Guide them to notice the use of categories and headings, the type of information under each heading, and the writing style.

Work together to write an animal profile. Copy the headings from "Animal Profiles" on the board or on an overhead transparency. Suggest that students write what they already know about the animal under the appropriate heading, using the same writing style as the author. Have students tell why they think the author chose this style of writing.

Then, invite the students to write a profile about an animal of their choice. Provide time for them to do their research. Students might share and publish their profiles
- on wall charts that they display and perhaps later bind in a big book with other writing from the unit.
- on smaller sheets that they add to a class binder or magazine.

For **Language Workshop — Spelling**, see page 16.

## Oral Communication

### Listen for Fabulous Facts

Choose one of the "Fabulous Facts" sections to read aloud. Have students listen so that at the end of the reading they can jot down three or four facts that they remember. Invite a few students to retell the facts they jotted. Talk with the students about ways to remember what they hear.

**Ways to remember what you hear**
- Think about key words.
- Place a finger on your desk each time you hear a point to remember.
- Jot down brief notes.
- Relate new information to something familiar.
- Think about what you heard that was fascinating, unique, or different from what you imagined.

 The homework project for Week 1 is to create an "animal facts" mini-booklet. See *Home Connections Newsletter*, Blackline Master 2.

Then, read other "Fabulous Facts" sections or ask pairs of students to read to each other. The listeners could share what they remember hearing and talk about strategies they used. To extend, students might gather fabulous facts about a new animal and tell these facts to others. They could make an audiotape of their presentation and add it to the classroom listening area so that other students might listen to it.

 See **Assess Learning**, page 15.

*Animal Profiles*

Students might use information in the "Food" and "Predators" sections of the profiles as a starting point for their food chains.

# Link to Curriculum

## Science

### Find Out About Food Chains

Invite small groups to create food chains for the animals in the profiles or for other animals of interest. Encourage students to explain how each link is dependent on the one before.

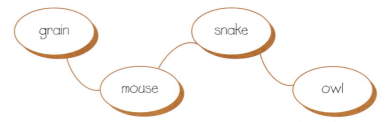

 Students could use a computer paint program such as *Super Paint 3.5 Deluxe* to draw the food chains. (See pages 5 and (ii) for more information.)

## Mathematics

### Create and Solve Mathematics Problems

Students could create mathematics problems based on information provided in the animal profiles. They can exchange their problems with a partner, and solve.

| | |
|---|---|
| If a black bear can travel 60 km/h, how far can it travel in 3 h? | If a monarch butterfly flies over 300 km/day, how far would it fly in one week? |
| A snowy owl eats more than 2 kg/day. About how many grams is that? | Is it possible, impossible, certain, or uncertain that a certain species of chameleon would live on Madagascar? |

## Language Arts

### Write an Animal Adventure Story

Have the students write an adventure story about an animal of their choice. They could model their story after a book they read or a movie or television program they saw. Encourage the students to make their stories as realistic as possible by thinking about the animal's appearance, behaviors, enemies, and habitat.

### Begin an Animal Word Bank

Pairs of students can skim the profiles to locate sentences with difficult or interesting words related to animals. They could read each sentence aloud to one another and discuss the meaning of the animal word, perhaps checking in a dictionary. Then, the students could begin an animal word bank by writing the word and its meaning on a card. Encourage them to add to their word bank throughout the unit.

> description: what something looks like

> condition: situation

> migration: moving to a new place when the seasons change

> adaptation: a change in what something looks like or how it acts to suit the environment

The students could use these word cards as a reference when reading or writing. They might
- keep the cards in envelopes or word boxes/cans.
- display the word cards on the wall or big book pages.
- arrange the word cards alphabetically or group them according to suggested categories.
- copy the words into personal dictionaries.
- use the cards to make animal word games.

> An inquiry unit exposes students to a large number of "technical" or topic-specific words. While it is not necessary for all these words to be part of the students' oral and written vocabularies, students will benefit from a working knowledge of the words.

## Assess Learning

### Oral Communication (see p. 13)

Use one of the "Fabulous Facts" listening passages as a **performance assessment** of each student's ability to assess information. To help students record their facts, prepare a worksheet similar to the one shown for recording and jotting down the facts.

Students could store their results as a **work sample** in their portfolios.

**Fabulous Facts**
Name of animal: _____
1. _____
2. _____
3. _____
4. _____
5. _____

A strategy I used to help me remember the facts is: _____

*Animal Profiles*

## Language Workshop — Spelling

*Blackline Master 21*

### Explore and Discover

Use Blackline Master 21 to make overhead transparency cards and to reproduce copies for students to use.

Review any words students are unsure of, then guide them in sorting the word cards into categories. Suggest that they first group words according to meaning, for example, animal words and words related to scenery. Then, they could sort the words in other ways.

Invite students to share their groupings. Discuss the common features and spelling patterns for plurals, focusing on the "-es" ending and irregular plurals.

Have students clap out the syllables to help them form the generalization about the plurals "foxes," "branches," "marshes,"and "bushes": add "-es" to the root word when the plural ending makes a separate syllable.

Have students suggest rhyming words, root words, or related words. Write these new words with the plural patterns on charts. Encourage students to add to the charts.

### Pretest

Administer the word list as a pretest, perhaps using the spelling buddy approach. Dictate the words, each time saying the word, using it in a sentence related to "Animal Profiles," and then repeating the word.

Collaboratively correct the words. Show each word, asking the students to put a dot under the letters they have spelled correctly, and underline places where they had errors. Students can list the words they need to study.

Students who have few or no errors could
- study Theme/Challenge words from the story.
- locate and practise challenging words from their own writing.
- play or create word games.
- act as spelling resource leaders for other students.

Students experiencing difficulties could
- be given fewer words or less difficult ones.
- study the Early words and other related pattern words (rhyming, same beginning letters, …).

**ANIMAL PROFILES**

- plurals: -s, -es, and -ies endings; irregular plurals

| eyes | mice | meadows | foxes |
| geese | cages | marshes | hours |
| bushes | butterflies | bodies | branches |

**Theme/Challenge Words**

- animal words

| hibernate | species | chrysalis |
| caterpillars | fierceness | |

**Early Words**

- wh pattern; sh pattern

| white | whale | when | fish | ship |

### Study and Practise

Students could
- use Learning Strategy Card 3 to study words identified after the pretest.
- highlight the pattern in each word on their study cards, and place the cards in piles according to these patterns in preparation for a riddle game. Students give a partner a one-sentence clue for the meaning of each word and identify the pattern. The partner identifies and spells the word.

### Post Test

Administer the post test. For those students who have an altered list, give the test at another time. Record the number of words each student spelled correctly and note the improvement since the pretest. Identify the types of errors students made for reteaching and study.

**SPELLING BUDDIES**

Pair students of like abilities and have them responsible for dictating to each other words for the pretests and post tests. Spelling buddies can help one another in checking the pretest, and in their study and practise.

# Desert Tortoise

This poem by Byrd Baylor describes the life of an old desert tortoise.

Anthology, pages 12–13
Blackline Masters 3 and 4
Learning Strategy Card 29

## Learning Choices

**LINK TO EXPERIENCE**

Web Desert Information

Read "The Hare and the Tortoise"

**READ AND RESPOND TO TEXT**

READING FOCUS
- read a variety of fiction and non-fiction materials for different purposes
- STRATEGY: **listen and visualize**

REVISIT THE TEXT

READING
Recognize First-Person Voice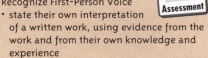
- state their own interpretation of a written work, using evidence from the work and from their own knowledge and experience

WRITING
Keep a Learning Log
- produce pieces of writing using a variety of specific forms

ORAL COMMUNICATION
Choral Read the Poem
- use appropriate tone of voice and gestures in social and classroom activities

**LINK TO CURRICULUM**

SCIENCE
Grow a Cactus Garden

LANGUAGE ARTS
Read Other Byrd Baylor Books

Develop Word Concepts and Wheels

MATHEMATICS
Graph Animals' Average Age Expectancies

THE ARTS
Create Desert Dioramas

### Key Learning Expectations

Students will
- read a variety of fiction and non-fiction materials for different purposes **(Reading Focus, p. 18)**
- state their own interpretation of a written work, using evidence from the work and from their own knowledge and experience **(Reading Mini Lesson, p. 18)**
- produce pieces of writing using a variety of specific forms (learning log) **(Writing Mini Lesson, p. 19)**
- use appropriate tone of voice and gestures in social and classroom activities **(Oral Communication Mini Lesson, p. 20)**

## LINK TO EXPERIENCE

### Web Desert Information

Have the students work in groups or as a whole class to brainstorm and web what they know about deserts. Encourage students to add to the web as they gather further information.

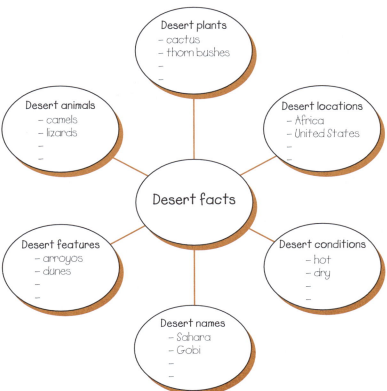

*Desert Tortoise* 17

## Read "The Hare and the Tortoise"

*Blackline Master 3*

Prepare an overhead transparency of "*The Hare and the Tortoise,*" Blackline Master 3, and/or duplicate copies for the students. Read and discuss the fable and the moral that is taught through one attribute of the tortoise. Invite students to share other information they know about tortoises.

# READ AND RESPOND TO TEXT

### Get Ready to Read

Read the title of the poem and the author's name. Have the students speculate and discuss what they might expect to hear or read about in a poem with this title. Students who are familiar with the author can share what they know about her writing.

## Reading Focus

Use a **listen and visualize** strategy. Read the poem aloud as the students listen and visualize the setting and the images.

Have students share the pictures they imagined. Read the poem aloud again, this time while the students follow along. Encourage them to find lines that helped create the pictures they saw. Students can read these lines aloud.

## Reader Response

Students could
- hold a conversation about the poem, using the following questions as a guide:
  – **What does the poet want to tell about desert tortoises?**
  – **How does the poet convey the tortoise's "oldness"?**
  – **How long do you think a desert tortoise might live?**
  – **Would you like to live in the desert? Why or why not?**
- draw the pictures they imagined during the readings.
- take turns reading aloud, in pairs, stanzas from the poem.
- add to the web they created in the Link to Experience. Some may wish to gather further information using electronic resources such as the *Life in the Desert* CD-ROM. (See pages 5 and (ii) for more information.)

# REVISIT THE TEXT

mini
LESSON

## Reading

## Recognize First-Person Voice

*Blackline Master 4*

Reread "Desert Tortoise." Ask the students who is speaking in the poem and what clues they used to identify the speaker. Elicit words used in first-person writing such as "I" and "our," pointing out that writing in first person allows the author to present information from the subject's perspective.

Blackline Master 4

18    *Collections 4*

To consolidate their understanding of first-person voice, the students could complete Blackline Master 4.

To extend the learning, students might identify the voice in favorite poems, stories, and narratives from the animal book display.

 See **Assess Learning**, page 22.

## Writing

### Keep a Learning Log

*Learning Strategy Card 29*

Share with the students information you learned while reading "Desert Tortoise," for example, what animals live in the desert. Using Learning Strategy Card 29, model how to record the information in a learning log.

- Write the date, explaining that this helps you remember when you learned something.
- Record the names of the desert animals mentioned in the poem, highlighting those you didn't know before.
- List questions you have about these animals.
- Write without stopping to proofread. Tell students that since the log is how you keep track of what you learned, it's more important to get all your ideas down first.

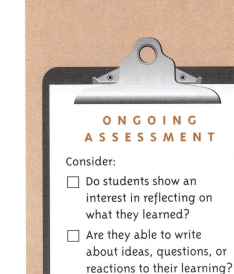

Then, have the students write in their learning logs for five to ten minutes about what they learned from "Desert Tortoise" about animals or the desert itself. Suggest that they share their entries with a partner and talk about how they might use learning logs in the future.

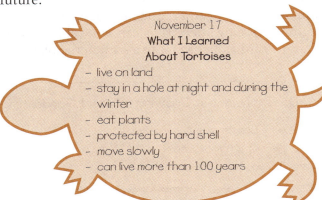

November 17
What I Learned About Tortoises
- live on land
- stay in a hole at night and during the winter
- eat plants
- protected by hard shell
- move slowly
- can live more than 100 years

For the duration of the unit, provide a designated time each day, perhaps at the beginning or end of the Language Arts class, for students to write in their learning logs.

### ONGOING ASSESSMENT

Consider:
- [ ] Do students show an interest in reflecting on what they learned?
- [ ] Are they able to write about ideas, questions, or reactions to their learning?
- [ ] Do they incorporate the features of a learning log in their writing?

*Desert Tortoise*

## Oral Communication

### Choral Read the Poem

Talk with the students about different ways to choral read a poem. (See *Choral Reading*, Learning Strategy Card 27, for a model.) Suggest two ways that might work well with this poem:
- The whole group could read the poem in unison.
- One student might read longer parts of the poem, while the rest of the group reads summative lines such as:
  - "I am the old one here."
  - "But tortoises grow old…lives stretch out."
  - "I know the slow sure way…how I fit in."
  - "I trust that shell…old tortoise to walk."

After students choose a way to read the poem, help them decide
- how they can use their voices to show the tortoise's oldness and slowness.
- whether actions or background music would enhance the reading.

The whole class might perform the choral reading together, or small groups could each plan their own presentation and share their reading with others. Encourage students to talk about the similarities and differences in the readings and to comment on how effectively each group conveyed the meaning of the poem.

## LINK TO CURRICULUM

### Science

#### Grow a Cactus Garden

As students plan a classroom desert garden, encourage them to identify what they know about desert plants and what questions they still have. They might visit a nursery or invite a family member who grows cacti to visit the class. Based on the information they gather, students could decide which plants to grow in their garden. They can write about the care of each plant on a card and attach it to a stick in the plant's pot.

---

**Questions About Growing a Desert Garden**

- What desert plants are there?
- Which ones would grow best in our classroom?
- How would we take care of them?

## Language Arts

### Read Other Byrd Baylor Books

After students read the biography of Byrd Baylor on page 13 of the anthology, suggest that they read other books that she has written. Students could respond to her writing by

- noting in their literature response journals similarities and differences between her books.
- tape-recording the book for the classroom listening area.
- painting a scene that her descriptive images bring to mind.
- writing a poem in free verse, imitating Byrd Baylor's style.

### BOOKS BY BYRD BAYLOR

*The Desert Is Theirs.* Aladdin, 1987.

*Desert Voices.* Aladdin, 1993.

*Hawk, I'm Your Brother.* Aladdin, 1986.

*Moon Song.* Simon & Schuster Children's, 1982.

*The Other Way to Listen.* Simon & Schuster Children's, 1978.

*Your Own Best Secret Place.* Simon & Schuster Children's, 1991.

### Develop Word Concepts and Wheels

Students might work in pairs or groups to develop concepts for old and slow. They could create word association wheels, or concept lists or books.

Desert Tortoise 21

## Mathematics

### Graph Animals' Average Age Expectancies

Students could each find the average age expectancy of one of the animals in the poem or of an animal of their choice. They might show these ages on a class bar graph and compare them with the average age expectancy of the desert tortoise.

## The Arts

### Create Desert Dioramas

Small groups or individuals might create a three-dimensional desert scene in a shoe box or on folded cardboard. They could include specific desert features as well as animals and plants they learned about in the poem and through their research.

# Assess Learning

### Reading (see p. 18)

Assess students' work based on *Who Is Speaking?*, Blackline Master 4, as a **work sample** of their ability to interpret text and apply what they know about voice in writing. Have students read their first-person pieces aloud in small groups. Select one group to assess and, with the group members, talk about questions such as:
- Did you use first-person pronouns (I, me, mine, my, we, ours, us, …) throughout your story or poem?
- Would your character use that vocabulary, that tone, and those types of sentences?
- Do you get the feeling that it is really the character speaking?

Assess the writing of students in other groups in the same way, or gather their writing and assess the pieces by reading them individually.

# Lily Pad Pond

Set in a woodland pond, Bianca Lavies' photo essay describes the growth of a tadpole and the many creatures it meets throughout its life.

Anthology, pages 14–17
Blackline Masters 5 and 21

## Learning Choices

**LINK TO EXPERIENCE**

Share Knowledge About Ponds
Listen to the Sounds of a Pond

**READ AND RESPOND TO TEXT**

READING FOCUS
- read a variety of fiction and non-fiction materials for different purposes
- STRATEGY: **double look**

**REVISIT THE TEXT**

READING
Create a Life-Cycle Diagram
- identify the main idea in a piece of writing, and provide supporting details

WRITING
Language Workshop — Style
- vary sentence structure
Language Workshop — Spelling
- compound words; words with re- prefix

VISUAL COMMUNICATION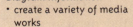
Diagram Information
- create a variety of media works

**LINK TO CURRICULUM**

LANGUAGE ARTS
Make a Pond Big Book
Generate Lists of Pond Words

SCIENCE
Study Pond Pictures

THE ARTS
Paint a Pond Mural

## Key Learning Expectations

Students will
- read a variety of fiction and non-fiction materials for different purposes **(Reading Focus, p. 24)**
- identify the main idea in a piece of writing, and provide supporting details **(Reading Mini Lesson, p. 24)**
- vary sentence structure **(Writing Mini Lesson, p. 25)**
- create a variety of media works (diagrams) **(Visual Communication Mini Lesson, p. 26)**

## LINK TO EXPERIENCE

### Share Knowledge About Ponds

Begin a pond display of books, magazines, pictures, and videotapes. Invite students to tell about their visits to a pond or to share what they know about ponds from print and non-print resources. As students talk about their pond experiences, listeners could close their eyes and imagine the sights, sounds, smells, and textures. Encourage students to add to the display as they read the selection.

### Listen to the Sounds of a Pond

Invite the students to listen closely to an audiotape or CD with sounds of a pond, for example, Dan Gibson's *Solitudes: Volume 4* (Solitudes, 1982). Ask them to identify what they heard. Depending on the season and your location, students could make their own tape of pond sounds, including an insert that identifies each sound. They might add the tape to the classroom listening area and invite other students to guess what made the sound. Students could check their guesses against the insert.

*Lily Pad Pond* 23

## Get Ready to Read

Ask the students to read the title and examine the photographs to identify what the selection will be about and to predict the kind of information they will read.

# Read and Respond to Text

### Reading Focus

Use a **double look** strategy. During the first reading, the students can focus on the flow of the story and on the activity in the pond. After they share their ideas on life in the pond, have them read the photo essay again to gather specific information about the various pond creatures. Encourage the students to jot down the names of the creatures, as well as one important fact about each of them. Discuss the selection, inviting students to share specific information they jotted down.

### Reader Response

Students could
- make a pond web centred around a lily pad, with the names and/or illustrations of all the creatures in the selection.
- share with a partner two or three fabulous facts they learned about a pond creature.
- tell about another pond animal they have seen or read about.
- write a poem about pond life, perhaps using Byrd Baylor's style.
- read aloud an interesting part of the essay to a partner.

# Revisit the Text

## Reading

### Create a Life-Cycle Diagram

Talk with the students about how the tadpole developed over time. Jot down what they remember about the specific changes that took place at each stage. Then, have the students skim the selection to confirm and/or change their recollections.

Using this information, help the students create headings for a circular diagram showing the development of the bullfrog. Discuss the concept of a life cycle and ask the students what they think will happen after the "great big bullfrog" stage.

Students could work in small groups to complete the life-cycle diagram, adding drawings for each stage as well as information about the changes.

To extend the activity, students may wish to make a life-cycle diagram for another creature in the selection.

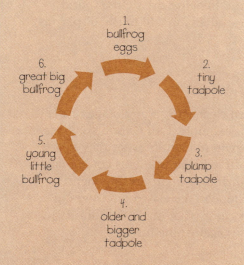

24   Collections 4

# Writing

## Language Workshop — Style

*Blackline Master 5*

To help the students develop an appreciation for how authors craft sentences, write these sentences on the board:
- page 14, *"A fat little tadpole lives among water lilies in a woodland pond."*
- page 15, *"As the tadpole gets older and bigger, her legs start to grow."*
- page 16, *"Up pops another turtle, a painted turtle, looking for a place to sit."*

Focus on the word order in the first sentence, helping the students see that it states who, what, and where. Elicit other ways to write the sentence by changing the word order. For example, students might suggest
- "Among water lilies in a woodland pond a fat little tadpole lives."
- "Among water lilies in a woodland pond lives a fat little tadpole."

Ask the students which version they like best, and why. Repeat the procedure for the remaining sentences.

To apply this, students could complete *Change the Order*, Blackline Master 5 and compare their work with a partner's.

To extend the activity, students could
- write sentences from other stories and change the word order to make these sentences more interesting.
- play the "Deal a Sentence" game in groups of four. The groups can create four stacks of cards with words or phrases on them: one stack that tells "who," one stack for "what," one for "where," and one for "when." The students should shuffle each stack and deal each person one card from each stack. The object is to create a sentence from the cards and change its order in as many ways as they can. Some of the sentences will be silly!

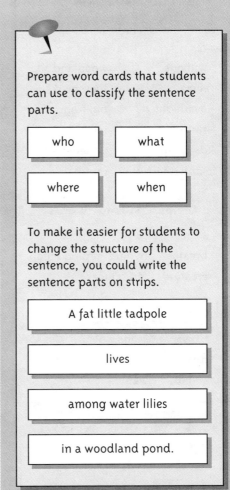

Prepare word cards that students can use to classify the sentence parts.

| who | what |
|---|---|
| where | when |

To make it easier for students to change the structure of the sentence, you could write the sentence parts on strips.

- A fat little tadpole
- lives
- among water lilies
- in a woodland pond.

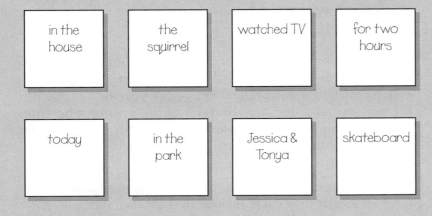

 See **Assess Learning**, page 29.

*Lily Pad Pond*

## LILY PAD POND

- compound words; words with re- prefix

  | without | woodland |
  |---|---|
  | remain | toothmarks |
  | overnight | bullfrog |
  | sunfish | recycle |
  | dragonfly | underwater |
  | sunbathe | return |

  **Theme/Challenge Words**

- animal words

  breathe   nymph   reproduction
  creature   reproduce

  **Early Words**

- consonant blends

  | dry | fly | plant |
  |---|---|---|
  | stand | want | |

Blank word cards are included on each spelling word blackline master. They can be used for
- personal words from the students' writing.
- Theme/Challenge or Early words from the selection.
- other related words (rhyming words, those with the same spelling pattern, derivatives, homonyms).

---

 **Language Workshop — Spelling**

• compound words; words with re- prefix

*Blackline Master 21*

### Explore and Discover

You can use Blackline Master 21 and the sort, share, discuss, and chart procedure outlined on page 16 to work with the words.

Have the students sort their word cards and share their groupings. Then, guide them to focus on the spelling or functional patterns of the words in the spelling list and other related words.

Invite students to brainstorm other words with the prefix "re-" and to use some of these in a sentence. Help students use the sentences to determine the meaning of the prefix "re-."

Follow this exploration and discovery with a **pretest**, **study and practise**, and a **post test** as outlined on page 16.

### Study and Practise

Students could
- use Learning Strategy Card 3 as a guide for studying words identified after the pretest.
- cut apart their compound word cards, shuffle them, and with a partner, combine the parts to make various compound words. They could first spell each compound word, then give a meaning.
- copy the words with prefixes. Under each, they could write the word again: once with a blank for the prefix and the second time with a blank for the root word. Then, they could fill in the blanks and spell the words.

```
remain
____main
re_____
```

## Visual Communication
### Diagram Information

Help the students retrieve and interpret the information in this text by suggesting that they collaboratively build a diagram. Begin by establishing the time frames—one year ago, after one year, and several years later—and the specific settings where the tadpole and the young bullfrog live—the water-lily stem and the log. Have the students begin their diagram by recording this information.

Then, encourage pairs to revisit the text and find additional information that they could include in their diagrams.

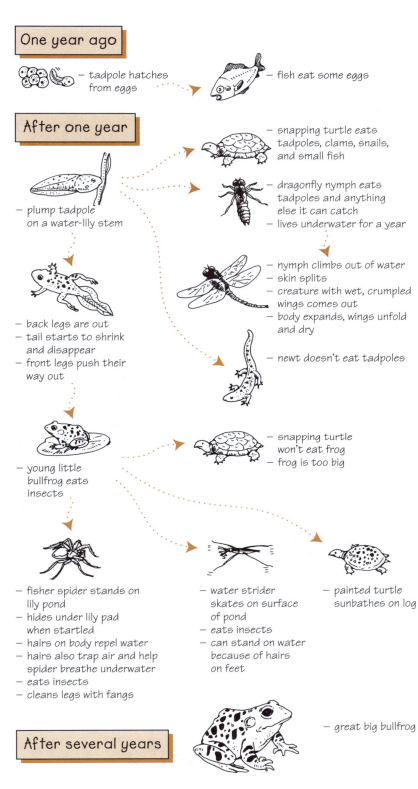

One year ago
- tadpole hatches from eggs
- fish eat some eggs

After one year
- plump tadpole on a water-lily stem
- snapping turtle eats tadpoles, clams, snails, and small fish
- dragonfly nymph eats tadpoles and anything else it can catch
- lives underwater for a year
- back legs are out
- tail starts to shrink and disappear
- front legs push their way out
- nymph climbs out of water
- skin splits
- creature with wet, crumpled wings comes out
- body expands, wings unfold and dry
- newt doesn't eat tadpoles
- young little bullfrog eats insects
- snapping turtle won't eat frog
- frog is too big
- fisher spider stands on lily pond
- hides under lily pad when startled
- hairs on body repel water
- hairs also trap air and help spider breathe underwater
- eats insects
- cleans legs with fangs
- water strider skates on surface of pond
- eats insects
- can stand on water because of hairs on feet
- painted turtle sunbathes on log

After several years
- great big bullfrog

Using the diagrams, students could
- retell the photo essay from the point of view of one of the pond animals.
- choose a favorite scene to illustrate.
- work in small groups to create a timeline or wall story of the information.

 See **Assess Learning**, page 29.

## USING DIAGRAMS TO INTERPRET CONTENT

This diagramming strategy will support students who

- tend to comprehend better by visualizing information.
- prefer to communicate by organizing content using graphic design elements.
- like to combine print and non-print literacies to make an integrated text.

This strategy is particularly significant in inquiry-based units such as science and social studies, and is one that students might wish to model as they present their own research.

One professional book that focuses on various diagramming strategies as well as other visual information strategies is *I Can See What You Mean: Children at Work with Visual Information* by Steve Moline (Pembroke Publishers, 1995). Many examples in this book are from Steve Moline's a.k.a. David Drew's *Informazing* materials, available from Prentice Hall Ginn.

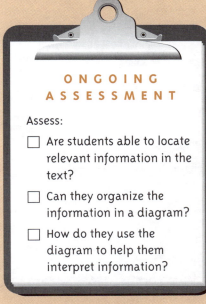

### ONGOING ASSESSMENT

Assess:
- ☐ Are students able to locate relevant information in the text?
- ☐ Can they organize the information in a diagram?
- ☐ How do they use the diagram to help them interpret information?

*Lily Pad Pond*

# Link to Curriculum

## Language Arts

### Make a Pond Big Book

Invite students to look at big books from the library to see how they are designed and what the illustrations add to the text. Then, encourage the class to make a big book about pond animals. Students could each write a "Who am I" riddle about a pond creature on the front of a page. On the back of the page, they could draw a picture of the animal and write its name. Students can share their class big book with younger children in the school.

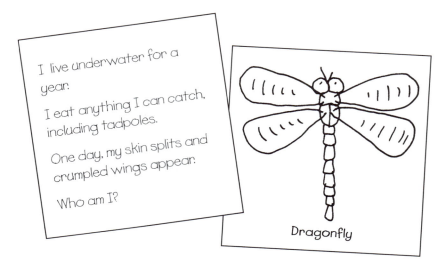

### Generate Lists of Pond Words

Invite students to jot down, on word cards or strips, pond words or phrases that come to mind. Other students, working in pairs or groups, could arrange the word cards or strips as a list poem. When students are satisfied with their poems, they could post them in the inquiry area or present them as a rhythmic verse.

## Science

### Study Pond Pictures

Encourage students to bring from home photos, slides, paintings, and magazines or books with pictures of pond life. Students could talk about what they see in the pictures and write the information they find on sentence strips. Suggest that students sort the information in different categories and create headings for each set of strips. Students might use these strips to write short descriptive paragraphs about pond life, which they could display with the pictures.

## The Arts

### Paint a Pond Mural

Have students plan a mural of a pond. As a group, they might list the animal and plant life that they would like to depict, then decide who will paint each part. Suggest that students research what they will be painting to ensure accurate representation. Students could add their mural to the pond life display.

If there is an outdoor area nearby, such as a pond or a forest, students may wish to visit and write about the animal life they observe there.

# Assess Learning

## Writing (see p. 25)

Assess each student's **work sample** on the blackline master to determine if they are able to offer variations in sentence structure. Note whether they can vary sentences
- at a practice level (questions 1–2).
- to respond to prompts (questions 3–5).
- to edit a piece of their own writing (question 6).

Hold a **personal conference** to discuss your assessment with any students you might be concerned about.

OR

## Visual Communication (see p. 26)

Assess students' ability to gather, organize, and represent information from text by first looking at their diagrams for accuracy and sequential flow of information. Then, look at how they used that information in their follow-up photo essay, illustration, timeline, or wall story. Again, check for accuracy of information and correct sequencing of events, as well as inclusion of important details.

*Lily Pad Pond*

# The Wounded Wolf

In her picture book story, Jean Craighead George tells of an injured wolf fighting for survival as predators await its death.

Anthology, pages 18–27
Blackline Masters 6, 7, and 22

## Learning Choices

**LINK TO EXPERIENCE**

Recall Information About Wolves
Ask Questions About Wolves

**READ AND RESPOND TO TEXT**

READING FOCUS
- read a variety of fiction and non-fiction materials for different purposes
- STRATEGY: **read, pause, and reflect**

**REVISIT THE TEXT**

READING
Diagram the Plot
- identify and describe elements of stories

WRITING
Write a Book Cover Synopsis
- communicate ideas and information for a variety of purposes and to specific audiences
Language Workshop — Spelling
- aw and au patterns; plurals: -ves ending

VISUAL COMMUNICATION
Mime the Story
- use appropriate gestures

**LINK TO CURRICULUM**

LANGUAGE ARTS
Write About Wolf Populations

SCIENCE
Hold a Question/Answer Quiz

THE ARTS
Set up a Wolf Display

## Key Learning Expectations

Students will
- read a variety of fiction and non-fiction materials for different purposes **(Reading Focus, p. 31)**
- identify and describe elements of stories (plot) **(Reading Mini Lesson, p. 32)**
- communicate ideas and information for a variety of purposes and to specific audiences (picture book story) **(Writing Mini Lesson, p. 32)**
- use appropriate gestures (mime) **(Visual Communication Mini Lesson, p. 34)**

## LINK TO EXPERIENCE

### Recall Information About Wolves

Show the students a picture of a wolf and ask what they know about this animal. Record their facts in a chart. Have students categorize the information under headings such as appearance, homes, food, enemies, and behavior, then invite them to represent the information in a web.

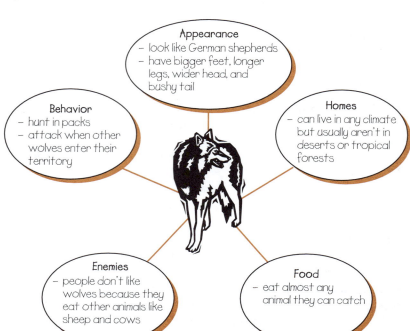

30  Collections 4

### Ask Questions About Wolves

Invite the students to write questions that they have about wolves on strips of paper. Post the strips in the inquiry area. The students could keep the questions in mind as they read the selection. Have them write on the back of the appropriate paper strips answers that they discover, as well as the related page references.

Interested students might bring in books about wolves from home or from the library and add them to the inquiry area. When they have time, they could use these resources and non-print resources such as encyclopedia CD-ROMs to research questions for which they couldn't find answers in "The Wounded Wolf." Have students write their answers and information sources on the back of the strips.

## READ AND RESPOND TO TEXT

### Reading Focus

*Blackline Master 6*

Use a **read, pause, and reflect** strategy. Read aloud or play the audio version of the first part of the story, pages 18–19. After the reading, invite the students to examine the illustration at the bottom of page 19. Ask what bird is pictured and why it is flying above a wounded wolf. Then, encourage the students to reflect on the first part of the story, using *Read, Pause, and Reflect Grid for The Wounded Wolf*, Blackline Master 6, as a guide.

The students could work in small groups to read or listen to the rest of the story in sections, pausing after each part to answer the questions and to confirm predictions they made.

### Reader Response

Students could
- hold a conversation about the story, using questions such as the following as a guide:
  – Did you like the story? Why? Why not?
  – How did the author make you feel what Roko was feeling?
  – How would you have acted in Roko's place?
  – Do you think the story would make a good movie? Why? Why not?
  – What did this story teach you about wolves that you didn't know before?
  – Did it change your impressions of wolves?
- read aloud lines from the story that show suspenseful moments.
- draw a picture of an exciting part of the story.
- reread the story with a partner to clarify some points.
- read other books by Jean Craighead George.

### Get Ready to Read

Have the students read the title and scan the illustrations to hypothesize about where the story takes places, how the wolf was wounded, and what might happen next. Suggest that they read to confirm their hypotheses.

**BOOKS BY JEAN CRAIGHEAD GEORGE**

*The Grizzly Bear with the Golden Ears.* HarperCollins, 1982.

*My Side of the Mountain.* Puffin, 1991.

*One Day in The Tropical Rain Forest.* HarperTrophy, 1995.

*The Wounded Wolf* 31

## ONGOING ASSESSMENT

Observe:
- ☐ Do students recognize the drama in each episode?
- ☐ Can they identify which episodes are part of the rising action, the climax, and the falling action?
- ☐ Are they able to draw a diagram to show the plot?

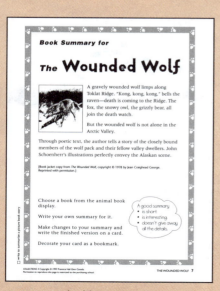

Blackline Master 7

# REVISIT THE TEXT

## Reading

### Diagram the Plot

Invite students to retell the events of the story. Write each event on an overhead transparency strip. Then, ask the students how they felt at different parts of the story. Have them identify times of uncertainty, tension, fear, relaxation, and relief.

Together, create an action pyramid to represent the level of suspense throughout the story. Use the strips to show the first few events in the rising action, the peak or the climax, and the first few events in the falling action.

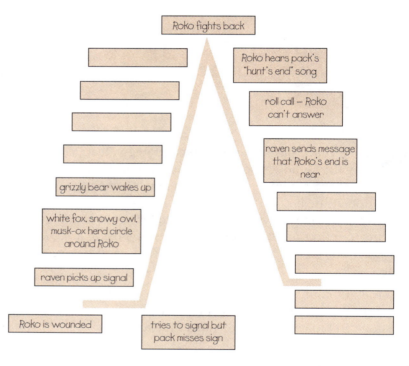

Have students work in small groups to complete the action pyramid, adding illustrations if they wish.

To extend the activity, students could diagram the plot of another animal adventure story that they have read.

## Writing

### Write a Book Cover Synopsis

*Blackline Master 7*

Show the students the book jacket summary from the original version of *The Wounded Wolf*, on Blackline Master 7. Invite them to look at other book summaries in the animal book display and to read aloud a few that catch their interest.

Together, list criteria for an effective story summary.

> A good story summary
> - is short.
> - tells you what the story is about without giving away all the details.
> - makes you want to read the book.

 Invite the students to write their own summaries for animal books in the classroom display that do not have summaries. Students could print the summaries on cards and place them inside the books as bookmarks. They might use computer graphics/text software, such as *The Print Shop Deluxe*, to design their bookmarks. (See pages 5 and (ii) for more information.)

## Language Workshop — Spelling

- aw and au patterns; plurals: -ves ending

*Blackline Master 22*

### Explore and Discover

You can use Blackline Master 22 and the sort, share, discuss, and chart procedure outlined on page 16 to work with the words.

Together, form a generalization about the "-ves" plurals. Note the homonym pair in the list and invite students to use each word in a sentence.

> I <u>pause</u> before I start reading my story to the class.
>
> The dog's <u>paws</u> are covered in mud.

Follow this exploration with a **pretest, study and practise,** and a **post test** as outlined on page 16.

### Study and Practise

Students could
- use Learning Strategy Card 3 as a guide for studying words identified after the pretest.
- prepare for a spelling quiz with a partner by looking at each word card, spelling the word quietly, and tracing over the spelling pattern with a colored marker. The partners could exchange cards and ask each other to spell the words.
- write their words inside two circles: one for verbs or action words and the other for nouns or naming words. They would then choose one tricky spelling word from each circle to illustrate, and write the word under the picture.

**THE WOUNDED WOLF**

- aw and au patterns; plurals: -ves ending

| pause | thawing | caused |
|-------|---------|--------|
| paws | hoof | wolf |
| dawn | hooves | crawls |
| wolves | drawing | leaves |

#### Theme/Challenge Words

- adventure words

| procession | celebration |
|------------|-------------|
| gnashes | deathwatch |
| ghostly | |

#### Early Words

- ck pattern

| pack | peck | picks |
|------|------|-------|
| rock | back | |

Ongoing reference charts can be made to record homonyms and irregular spellings as they are encountered in students' reading and writing.

*The Wounded Wolf*

## Visual Communication

### Mime the Story

Have the students read pages 18–19 to identify Roko's actions as he moves up the mountain. For example, they might say that he "limps," "pulls himself toward the shelter rock," "glances down the valley," "droops his head," and "stiffens his tail."

Invite volunteers to mime the actions while the rest of the group observes and comments on specific movements that make the mimes real. Then, arrange the students in groups to prepare pantomimes for other scenes in the story. Challenge each group to plan their scene by reading the text and focusing on particular actions of the animals. The may also decide to have a narrator read the part of the story as they mime the actions.

Students might mime
- the beginning of the hunt call scene on pages 20—21.
- Roko fighting back on page 23.
- the roll call scene on page 24.
- Roko's healing on pages 26—27.

Encourage students to present their mimes to the rest of the class. Then, talk about the mimes, eliciting that the author's strong use of action words helped the students identify actions.

 Interested groups could "polish" their mimes and present the scenes to another class, in the order they happened. Several students could narrate the dramatization, or they might play the COLLECTIONS 4 audio version during their presentation.

 See **Assess Learning**, page 35.

## LINK TO CURRICULUM

### Language Arts

### Write About Wolf Populations

Students can locate information in print and non-print resources about what is happening to the North American wolf population, and why. They could discuss the situation in small groups and brainstorm ideas about what could be done to preserve wolf populations and to reintroduce wolves to their native habitats.

Students may wish to address their letters to the fish and wildlife department of their provincial ministry of natural resources.

Encourage students to record their ideas on chart paper. They can then use their notes as the basis for a paragraph about their opinions of the situation and what can be done about it. Students could display their paragraphs in the hallway for others to read, or they might incorporate them in a letter to a group concerned with the future of wolves.

## Science

### Hold a Question/Answer Quiz

Students can use the question strips they made in the Link to Experience as the basis for a question/answer quiz. One student could act as game leader, asking two teams of students, in turn, the questions. In case of dispute, the leader could verify the answers by checking the sources listed on the back of the strips.

## The Arts

### Set up a Wolf Display

Students may wish to collect items that show the wolf in art and culture: prints, photographs, models, soap carvings, drawings, folktales, and picture books. They might also create wolf art pieces or stories, and write information cards describing how the wolf is portrayed in their artifacts and creations. They could display their materials in the school library.

**BOOKS ABOUT WOLVES**

*Dream Wolf*. Paul Goble. Simon & Schuster Children's, 1990.

*Lon Po Po: A Red Riding Hood Story from China*. Ed Young. Philomel Books, 1989.

*The Moon of the Gray Wolves*. Jean Craighead George. HarperCollins, 1991.

*Peter and the Wolf*. Sergei Prokofiev. Puffin, 1986.

*The True Story of the Three Little Pigs*. Jon Scieszka. Viking Children's Books, 1989.

# Assess Learning

## Visual Communication (see p. 34)

Arrange the students in small groups to **peer-assess** the mimes. Decide on and post the **criteria**, which could be similar to those shown.

As each group presents its mime, the other groups could use the criteria to assess the presentation.

Provide time for the groups to share their assessments and to offer suggestions to the presenting group.

You could complete an asssessment as well, recording your comments anecdotally for future reference.

---

**Criteria for Mime Group Presentation**

**MEANING**
- The mimes are true to the action of the story.
- Each student in the group
  - tells the story without speaking.
  - concentrates on the role.
  - uses specific movements that are mentioned in the text.
  - adds other movements appropriate to the animal.

**NARRATOR**
The narrator
- reads with expression.
- reads loudly and clearly.
- looks at the audience.

**RATING**
We would rate this group presentation as
1  2  3  4  5
Our reasons: _____

---

*The Wounded Wolf*

# THEME: ANIMALS IN THE WILD

**Anthology, pages 28–29**
Audio reading

> **Wetlands Essay** — *an essay*
> **Kerloo, Ker-lee-oo** — *a factual narrative*
> **The Sea Otter** — *a poem*

## STUDENT WRITING

### LINK TO THE THEME

After reading the selections, students could

- listen to the audio version and record in their learning logs what they learned about animals in the wild.
- talk with a partner about the different forms of student writing in this section and how each form conveys factual information.

### LINK TO THE WRITING PROCESS

**Write an Informational Poem**

Select students to read aloud the selections "Kerloo, Ker-lee-oo" and "Sea Otter," while the others listen to note how facts about animals are woven into the selections. Invite students to write an informational poem about an animal they researched or read about.

**Language Workshop — Grammar**

- use connecting words correctly to link ideas (e.g., if, because, without)

*Blackline Master 8*

#### Teach/Explore/Discover

Read aloud "Wetlands Essay." Talk with the students about how Joseph convinces readers of the importance of wetlands. Write on the board or on chart paper some of the points he raises. Focus on the language that Joseph uses to introduce or support his arguments,

underlining words such as "if," "because," and "without." Have students locate other sentences with these words and talk about how they help Joseph present his argument.

> <u>If</u> wetlands are destroyed, more floods will occur…
>
> The wetlands that cover North America should be conserved <u>because</u> they are very helpful to towns and cities near them.
>
> <u>Without</u> the wetlands these animals would die…

#### Practise/Apply

Students could
- complete *Giving Examples and Reasons*, Blackline Master 8.
- look in the selection for other words that introduce or support arguments.

### LINK TO THE WRITER

Students can read what Joseph says about drawing illustrations for his stories. They could draw a picture to accompany part of his essay or illustrate the informational poem they wrote in Link to the Writing Process.

36 *Collections 4*

# From A Whale-Watcher's Diary

In this excerpt from *In the Company of Whales*, Alexandra Morton chronicles her observations during a whale watch.

Anthology, pages 30–38
Blackline Masters 9, 10, 11–12, and 22      Learning Strategy Card 30

## Key Learning Expectations

Students will
- state their own interpretation of a written work, using evidence from the work and from their own knowledge and experience **(Reading Focus, p. 38)**
- read a variety of fiction and non-fiction materials for different purposes **(Reading Mini Lesson, p. 38)**
- choose words that are most effective for their purpose (verbs, adjectives) **(Writing Mini Lesson, p. 39)**
- create a variety of media works (observation record) **(Visual Communication Mini Lesson, p. 40)**

## Learning Choices

**LINK TO EXPERIENCE**

Display Knowledge About Whales

Discuss Observation Experiences

**READ AND RESPOND TO TEXT**

READING FOCUS
- state their own interpretation of a written work, using evidence from the work and from their own knowledge and experience
- STRATEGY: **guided listen and read**

**REVISIT THE TEXT**

READING
Make an Outline
- read a variety of fiction and non-fiction materials for different purposes

WRITING
Language Workshop — Style
- choose words that are most effective for their purpose
Language Workshop — Spelling
- be- pattern; oi and oy patterns

VISUAL COMMUNICATION
Make and Record Observations
- create a variety of media works

**LINK TO CURRICULUM**

LANGUAGE ARTS
Read About Tracking Technology

MATHEMATICS
Record Time Using the 24-hour Clock

THE ARTS
Prepare a Radio Phone Report

Listen to Environmental Music

## LINK TO EXPERIENCE

### Display Knowledge About Whales

Invite students to share what they know about whales and, if possible, to tell where they learned the information. Students could write their whale facts on card strips and display them on the chalkboard ledge, bulletin board, or in pocket charts.

> Whales aren't fish, they're mammals.

> Blue whales are the biggest whales.

### Discuss Observation Experiences

Talk with students about occasions when they observed something over a period of time. They might recall watching
- the growth of a plant from seed to mature plant.
- the activity of birds around a bird feeder.
- the appearance of the sky.

Ask students about some of the changes they noticed, eliciting that they had to watch carefully and consistently to observe details. Discuss the value of direct observation in obtaining accurate and reliable information, and talk about how it can be used to find out about an animal in its natural habitat.

*From A Whale-Watcher's Diary*

## Get Ready to Read

Have the students read the title and discuss what they know about diaries—what a diary is for, if they know someone who keeps one, ... Then, ask students to scan this diary to see how it seems to be organized and what kind of information it might contain. Invite the students to read or listen to the selection to see if their first impressions are accurate.

### BOOKS ABOUT WHALES

*I Wonder If I'll See a Whale*. Frances Ward Weller. Putnam, 1995.

*Rescue of the Stranded Whales*. Kenneth Mallory and Andrea Conley. Simon & Schuster, 1989.

*Siwiti — A Whale's Story*. Alexandra Morton. Orca, 1991.

*The Story of Three Whales*. Giles Whittell. Douglas & McIntyre, 1988.

*The Whale's Song*. Dyan Sheldon. Dial Books, 1991.

# READ AND RESPOND TO TEXT

## Reading Focus

*Blackline Master 9*

Using a **guided listen and read** strategy, small groups could read and respond to one section of text at a time. At the end of each section, they could talk about the questions on *Guided Reading Grid for From a Whale-Watcher's Diary*, Blackline Master 9, and clarify difficult concepts and vocabulary.

As a variation on this strategy, some groups could follow along in their anthologies as they listen to the audio version of the selection.

## Reader Response

Students could
- listen to the audio version, jotting down key words for five pieces of information they learned.
- sketch a new piece of information and share it with a friend.
  - gather other information about whales from print and non-print resources such as the CD-ROM *In the Company of Whales*. (See pages 5 and (ii) for more information.)
- draw a labelled diagram of a whale, showing its dorsal fin, pectoral fin, fluke, and other interesting features.
- talk with a partner about what it would be like to live on a floating house like the author and her son.

# REVISIT THE TEXT

## Reading

### Make an Outline

Ask the students to reread the boxed information on page 37 on their own or to listen to the audio version. Alternatively, you might choose volunteers to read the information aloud. Invite students to talk about what they learned.

To help the students classify the information, write the headings Definitions, How Echolocation Works, and Uses for Echolocation on chart paper or on an overhead transparency. Guide the students to place their information under the appropriate heading to make an outline. Add subheadings where helpful.

Suggest that students might include letters or numbers by the headings and points to make the outline easier to follow.

38   Collections 4

### A. Definitions
1. acoustic: depends on the use of sound
2. echolocation: locating objects with echoes

### B. How Echolocation Works
1. like a sound flashlight
2. whale can find out what's around
   (a) it sends out lots of clicks, moving its head so clicks go all over
   (b) clicks hit something and bounce back
   (c) different objects have different echoes
3. whales use echolocation to look up close
   (a) shorter and more clicks
   (b) can see parts better

### C. Uses of Echolocation
1. whales need to know if a female is carrying a calf
2. whales send out strong sounds to stun fish so they're slow enough to catch

Students could work in small groups to make an outline for "How Whales Get Their Names" or for an informational passage on whales in another book.

## Writing

### Language Workshop — Style

*Blackline Master 10*

Prepare Blackline Master 10 as an overhead transparency and duplicate it for the students. Focus on sentences 1–4, helping students identify what makes the descriptions effective and how the descriptions help them see pictures in their minds. Students may suggest that the author paints pictures by using

- specific descriptive words—*pale green* water, *melting* glaciers, sky is *deep red and orange*.
- strong action words—*zig-zag* up the inlet, *lunging* out of the water.

To apply their learning, students could
- complete Blackline Master 10.
- find other examples of descriptive sentences in their own writing and in the anthology, possibly recording their favorites in their literature response journals. Encourage students to underline the parts of each sentence that are especially descriptive.

> Air <u>erupted</u> from the blowhole like a volcano.
>
> The winds were <u>whipping</u> up the waves.

## ONGOING ASSESSMENT

Assess:
- ☐ Do students understand how echolocation works?
- ☐ Can they organize their information under main headings?
- ☐ Are they able to make an outline for other information?

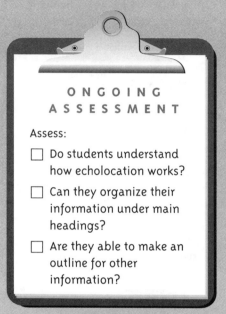

Blackline Master 10

*From A Whale-Watcher's Diary*

### FROM A WHALE-WATCHER'S DIARY

- be- pattern; oi and oy patterns

| noises | oil | because |
| began | moist | beneath |
| joins | joy | behave |
| behind | voice | pointer |

**Theme/Challenge Words**

- whale study words

identification echolocation
acoustic hydrophone
research

**Early Words**

- long e patterns: ee and ea

| sleep | seem | hear |
| each | lead | |

 The homework project for Week 2 is to make an observation record. See *Home Connections Newsletter*, Blackline Master 2.

## Language Workshop — Spelling

• be- pattern; oi and oy patterns

*Blackline Master 22*

### Explore and Discover

You can use Blackline Master 22 and the sort, share, discuss, and chart procedure outlined on page 16 to work with the words.

Follow this exploration with a **pretest, study and practise,** and a **post test** as outlined on page 16.

### Study and Practise

Students could
- use Learning Strategy Card 3 as a guide for studying words identified after the pretest.
- sort their study cards into piles according to spelling patterns and arrange each pile in alphabetical order. They can ask a partner to check their order.
- choose five of the trickiest words from their study cards and write each one with a thick wax crayon. Then, as they trace each word, they should gently scrape each letter with their fingernail, a dull pencil, or a paper clip.

## Visual Communication

### Make and Record Observations

*Learning Strategy Card 30*

Have the students brainstorm something that is happening in their environment, possibly connected to their animal investigations, that they could observe over time. They may suggest watching

- the eating habits or movements of a classroom pet.
- developments in an aquarium filled with pond life.
- the sprouting of crops in a field or seeds in a container.
- a bird building a nest.

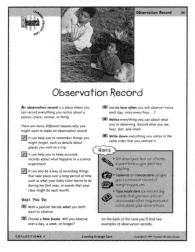

Using Learning Strategy Card 30 as a guide, talk with the students about how they can make careful observations of one of these events. Suggest that they look at their subject from different perspectives and search for the unusual and for details they may not have noticed before. Discuss how students might record their observations using notes, labelled diagrams, and illustrations.

40  Collections 4

Then, encourage the students to choose an object, place, or person from the brainstormed list to observe over a period of time and to write about what they see in an observation record. Students may wish to carry out their observations at home.

| Day | Time | What I observed |
|---|---|---|
| Monday | 8:45 a.m. | Two workers cleared away all the extra gravel with shovels and short brooms with bristles. One was a man and one was a woman. |
|  | 9:15 a.m. | A city truck came by and two more men joined the crew. Before the truck left, they unloaded a jackhammer. The driver got out and talked to one of the men who had a shovel. |

 See **Assess Learning**, page 42.

# LINK TO CURRICULUM

## Language Arts

### Read About Tracking Technology

*Blackline Masters 11–12*

Interested students might reread Alexandra Morton's 0740 diary entry (pp. 31–32), which describes how she uses a hydrophone in her work, and predict how hydrophones are used with cellular telephones to track the movements of whales. Small groups could read Blackline Masters 11–12 to confirm their predictions. Some students might search for other articles that describe different technologies used to study endangered animals.

## Mathematics

### Record Time Using the 24-hour Clock

Encourage students to reread the explanation on page 30 about how to convert to the 24-hour clock. Students might use the 24-hour clock to
- record the times of specific events during the day, such as recess or the beginning of a favorite television program.
- rewrite the times in their observation records.
- track a day on the weekend.

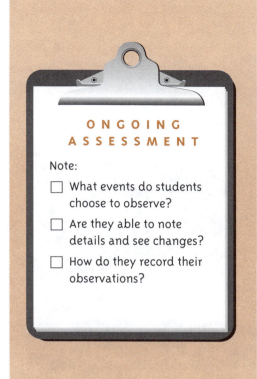

## ONGOING ASSESSMENT

Note:
- ☐ What events do students choose to observe?
- ☐ Are they able to note details and see changes?
- ☐ How do they record their observations?

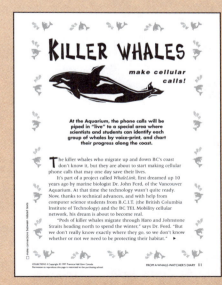

Blackline Masters 11–12

*From A Whale-Watcher's Diary*

## The Arts

### Prepare a Radio Phone Report

Small groups could role-play a scene in which they portray whale-watchers using a radio phone to report their sightings. Students could base their reports on Alexandra Morton's diary entries, or write their own reports, using information gathered from personal experiences or from other print and non-print resources. Encourage them to decide who in their group will report each sighting and whether to add sound effects. Students could tape-record their reports for others to listen to.

### Listen to Environmental Music

Students could listen to tapes of environmental music that feature the sounds of the ocean, of whales, or of dolphins. They might write a story or poem inspired by the music, or paint or draw a picture related to the sounds they hear.

## Assess Learning

### Visual Communication (see p. 40)

Use the students' Observation Records as a **work sample** of a viewing assignment that they completed independently.

- Hold a quick work-in-progress conference with each student to assess the suitability of the topic that he or she chose and to answer any questions with respect to the assignment. Encourage students to tell you their work plan for how and when they will complete the task.
- Assess the completed reports:
  – Were the observations concrete and specific?
  – Did they include details?
  – Were the details from more than one perspective?
  – Were they unusual in any way?
  – Did the students include diagrams or illustrations to further explain their points?

Place the completed Observation Records in the students' portfolios. Encourage them to include a **reflective comment** on the activity, telling
- how they felt about the task.
- whether they were able to stick to their work plan.
- what they would do differently next time.

# Animal Crimes, Animal Clues

In her article, Leslie Dendy describes how forensic scientists help track down wildlife criminals.

Anthology, pages 39–45
Blackline Master 23
Learning Strategy Card 31

## Learning Choices

**LINK TO EXPERIENCE**

Tell About Crimes Against Animals

Brainstorm Detective Words

**READ AND RESPOND TO TEXT**

READING FOCUS
- identify the main idea in a piece of writing, and provide supporting details
- STRATEGY: read, paraphrase, and teach

**REVISIT THE TEXT**

READING
Read Captions
- read a variety of fiction and non-fiction materials for different purposes

WRITING
Write a Paragraph
- organize and develop ideas using paragraphs
Language Workshop — Spelling
- f, ff, and ph patterns

VISUAL COMMUNICATION
Use a Microscope or Magnifying Glass
- analyze media works

**LINK TO CURRICULUM**

LANGUAGE ARTS
Make Animal Crime Cards

SCIENCE
Research Crime-Solving Instruments

THE ARTS
Compose a Song

## Key Learning Expectations

Students will
- identify the main idea in a piece of writing, and provide supporting details **(Reading Focus, p. 44)**
- read a variety of fiction and non-fiction materials for different purposes **(Reading Mini Lesson, p. 45)**
- organize and develop ideas using paragraphs **(Writing Mini Lesson, p. 45)**
- analyze media works (magnifying glass) **(Visual Communication Mini Lesson, p. 47)**

## LINK TO EXPERIENCE

### Tell About Crimes Against Animals

Ask students whether they've ever witnessed a crime against an animal, or heard or read about one in the news. After they talk about the crimes, encourage students to think about who solves them and how. Record their ideas on chart paper and suggest that they revise the list or add to it as they read the selection.

### Brainstorm Detective Words

Invite students to brainstorm words that are associated with crimes and detectives. Record their suggestions in a web, encouraging them to add to the web as they learn new vocabulary from "Animal Crimes, Animal Clues."

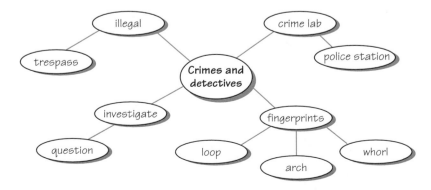

*Animal Crimes, Animal Clues*

## Get Ready to Read

Introduce the selection by reading page 39 to the students as they follow along. Talk about the meaning of "forensics," and ask students to use the definition, illustration, and title to predict what the article will be about. Have them flip through the selection, reading the headings and looking at the photographs, to make an early check on their predictions.

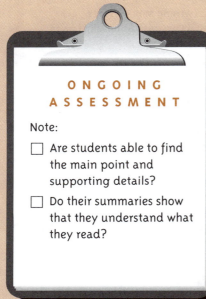

### ONGOING ASSESSMENT

Note:
- [ ] Are students able to find the main point and supporting details?
- [ ] Do their summaries show that they understand what they read?

## Read and Respond to Text

### Reading Focus

Use a variation of the read and paraphrase strategy—**read, paraphrase, and teach**. Assign groups different sections of the article to read. Group members could read their section silently, then discuss what they learned and ask questions to clarify anything they didn't understand. Then, they could
- identify the main point and record it in a chart.
- list important details.
- summarize what they learned in a few sentences.

| Title of section | Main point | Important details |
|---|---|---|
| Which weapon? | • some people hunt deer with rifles and that's illegal | • hunting with bows and arrows is legal<br>• can check whether someone has used a rifle by looking for dust on suspect's hands |

Summary:

Have the groups take turns presenting their information to one another, and post their charts for reference. With this overall view of the selection, students can independently read the whole article to learn more.

### Reader Response

Students could
- hold a conversation about the article, using questions such as the following as a guide:
  - **What parts of the article surprised you?**
  - **How did the photographs help you understand the text?**
  - **What other features helped you understand difficult vocabulary?**
  - **Would you like to be a forensic scientist? Why? Why not?**
- write about the section they found most interesting.
- list four crimes from the article that people have committed against animals.
- note words they were unsure of and check them in a dictionary or thesaurus.
- read more about measures taken to stop crimes against animals.

 See **Assess Learning**, page 49.

44  Collections 4

# REVISIT THE TEXT

## Reading

### Read Captions

Have students reread the section "Ivory Alibis" on pages 42–43, then focus their attention on the caption at the bottom of page 42. Initiate a discussion about what the caption adds to the text and how it helps readers. Elicit that captions

- are easy to understand because they're short, concise, and related to illustrations or photographs.
- highlight main points in the text.
- support the text by providing extra information and giving specific examples.
- may give clues for where readers can look for more detailed information.

As students read other captions in this selection, they can note what the captions add to the text and how they help readers. They might write a caption for the photograph on page 44 or for the photos in "Lily Pad Pond" (*Fur, Feathers, Scales, and Skin*, p. 14).

To extend the activity, suggest that students use this strategy when writing their own informational reports.

## Writing

### Write a Paragraph

*Learning Strategy Card 31*

Ask students what they know about a paragraph. Then, use Learning Strategy Card 31 as a guide for developing a paragraph based on one of the students' summary charts from the Reading Focus. Identify parts of the chart that would be the title of the paragraph, the topic sentence, the supporting details, and the conclusion. Use different-colored markers to highlight the parts.

On the board or overhead transparency, work with the students to write the main idea and important details as full sentences. Explain that this forms the main body of the paragraph. Talk about ways to conclude or summarize the information and write the final sentence. Then, decide on the title—either the one from the selection or a title of your own.

Encourage students to read the paragraph silently and suggest any changes. When the paragraph is complete, highlight the four parts according to the colors on the chart. ▶

*Animal Crimes, Animal Clues*

To apply their learning, students could write a four-part color-coded paragraph based on another chart. Encourage them to check that their paragraph includes
- a title.
- a main idea or topic sentence.
- detail sentences that support, explain, prove, or describe the main idea.
- a concluding sentence that could
  – repeat or restate the topic sentence.
  – ask a question.
  – state cause and effect.
  – make a hopeful statement.
  – express an opinion.

**Assessment** See **Assess Learning**, page 49.

### ANIMAL CRIMES, ANIMAL CLUES

- f, ff, and ph patterns

| officer | profit |
| photo | wildlife |
| elephants | giraffe |
| microphone | dolphin |
| stuff | found |
| fingerprints | telephone |

#### Theme/Challenge Words

- crime solution words

| microscope | detective |
| forensics | laboratory |
| photographer | |

#### Early Words

- consonant digraphs and blends

| snake | crime | while |
| shape | stripe | |

For future reference and practice, word cards can be stored in envelopes, in a personal dictionary or file box, in pockets inside students' journals, or taped to students' desks.

46  Collections 4

**Language Workshop — Spelling** • f, ff, and ph patterns

*Blackline Master 23*

### Explore and Discover

You can use Blackline Master 23 and the sort, share, discuss, and chart procedure outlined on page 16 to work with the words.

Follow this exploration with a **pretest, study and practise**, and a **post test** as outlined on page 16.

### Study and Practise

Students could
- use Learning Strategy Card 3 as a guide for studying words identified after the pretest.
- draw a line around each word to show its configuration and circle the "f" pattern.

- write each of their study words three times, putting a blank in place of letters that present difficulty. Then, they could fill in the blanks and think of ways that will help them remember the correct spelling of some of the words.

```
o _ _ i _ er
o _ _ i _ er
o _ _ i _ er
```
officer: The officer is off duty.

# Visual Communication
## Use a Microscope or Magnifying Glass

Brainstorm with the students instruments that people use to make objects look bigger. Invite them to demonstrate with equipment such as overhead projectors, slide projectors, magnifying glasses, binoculars, or opera glasses.

Show the students a photograph, slide, or overhead transparency of an object that has been magnified. Ask them what details they notice and compare this with what they would see with the naked eye. Discuss when people might use magnification instruments and note students' ideas in a web.

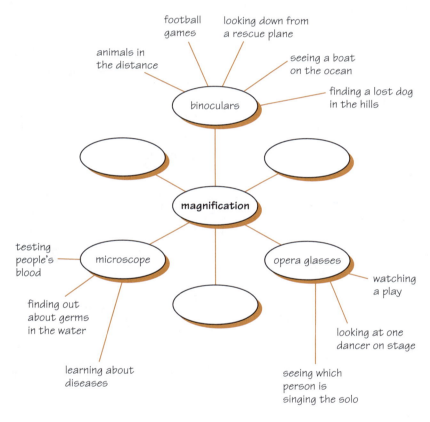

To apply the learning, set up microscopes, magnifying glasses, and binoculars around the classroom, along with various objects to be viewed such as flower petals, feathers, salt, and bread crumbs soaked in water. Provide time for students to visit the viewing areas at a specific time during the day, or you might set out a few items each day for the students to view after they have finished other work. Students can fill out observation sheets on which they draw or write what the object usually looks like and how it looks when it's magnified.

To extend the learning, students could invite people from the community who use magnifying objects as part of their job—lab technicians, veterinarians, doctors—to visit the class and demonstrate and talk about what they do.

*Animal Crimes, Animal Clues* 47

# Link to Curriculum

## Language Arts

### Make Animal Crime Cards

Invite pairs of students to design animal crime cards using information from the article and other resources. Students could include a picture of the animal, a description of the crime, and an explanation of how to solve the crime. They might create a display of their cards or use them to play a game that they've designed.

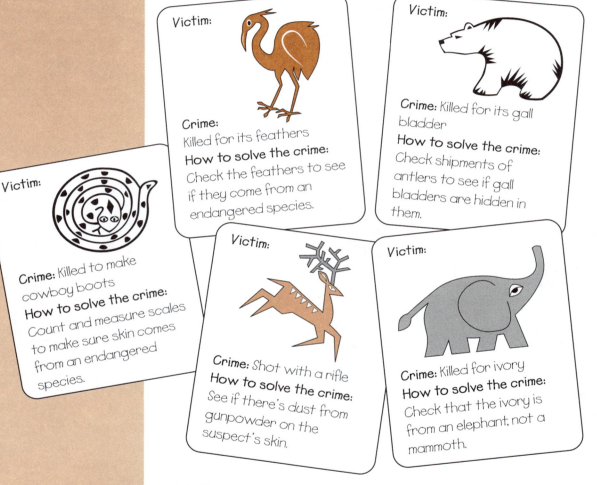

## Science

### Research Crime-Solving Instruments

Invite students to skim the article and note different instruments used to solve animal crimes. They could choose one of these instruments, or another that they have heard about, and find out more about how it works and when it is used. Encourage students to draw and label a diagram of the instrument, and write a brief description using the information they gathered. They could add their work to the unit bulletin board.

## The Arts

### Compose a Song

Small groups might write lyrics for a song about stopping crimes against wildlife. They could sing their song to a familiar tune, adding different effects and instrumentation to emphasize their message. Encourage students to rehearse their song, perhaps tape-recording it before singing it for the rest of the class.

## Assess Learning

### Reader Response (see p. 44)

Plan time to assess the response activity that the students chose. To prepare for the assessment, students could complete a **self-assessment** using a *Reader Response Activity Sheet*. (A blackline master of this sheet appears in the COLLECTIONS 4 Assessment Handbook.)

**Reader Response Activity Sheet**

Date: _____ Name: _____
Selection: _____
Activity I chose: _____
Why I chose it: _____
How I think I did on it: _____
How my teacher thinks I did on it: _____

OR

### Writing (see p. 45)

Assess the paragraph that the students wrote, using the **criteria** established on *Writing a Paragraph,* Learning Strategy Card 31. The example of student writing shown is at the expected level for Grade 4.

*by Tish*

Feather Findings

Beth Ann Sabo can catch people who kill birds by looking at feathers. Some peopk kill birds to get their beutiful feathers. Some people kill birds because they eat sheep and cattle. If Beth Ann finds a feather she can check it and salv a crime.

*Animal Crimes, Animal Clues*

# The Northern Way

This article, written by Michael Kusugak, describes the Inuit's respect for the animals on which they depend for food and clothing.

Anthology, pages 46–49
Blackline Masters 13 and 23
Learning Strategy Card 32

## Learning Choices

**LINK TO EXPERIENCE**

Reflect on Why People Hunt

Recall Information About the Inuit

**READ AND RESPOND TO TEXT**

READING FOCUS
- begin to develop research skills
- STRATEGY: **read and reflect**

REVISIT THE TEXT

READING
Find Answers in Text
- read a variety of fiction and non-fiction materials for different purposes

WRITING
Write a Group Report
- produce pieces of writing using a variety of specific forms
Language Workshop — Spelling
- gh pattern; -ful ending; superlatives

ORAL COMMUNICATION
Listen for Details
- express and respond to ideas and opinions concisely and clearly

**LINK TO CURRICULUM**

THE ARTS
Make an Animal Print

SCIENCE
Write an Animal Profile

LANGUAGE ARTS
Create a Glossary

Read About the Inuit

## Key Learning Expectations

Students will
- begin to develop research skills (title and text relationship) **(Reading Focus, p. 51)**
- read a variety of fiction and non-fiction materials for different purposes **(Reading Mini Lesson, p. 51)**
- produce pieces of writing using a variety of specific forms (report) **(Writing Mini Lesson, p. 52)**
- express and respond to ideas and opinions concisely and clearly **(Oral Communication Mini Lesson, p. 54)**

## LINK TO EXPERIENCE

### Reflect on Why People Hunt

Ask students to consider different reasons why people hunt. Encourage them to use what they learned in "Animal Crimes, Animal Clues" (*Fur, Feathers, Scales, and Skin*, p. 39) as a starting point, then elicit other possibilities including hunting for food, clothing, shelter, and sport.

### Recall Information About the Inuit

 Invite students to share what they know about the Inuit people and their lifestyle. Begin a list on chart paper, perhaps categorizing the information under headings such as "family life," "food," "transportation," and "culture." Students could add to the list as they gather more information from this article and other resources, including the Internet and encyclopedia CD-ROMs.

### About the Inuit

| Family Life | Food | Transportation | Culture |
|---|---|---|---|
| — parents teach children how to hunt and fish | — expensive groceries<br>— hunt and fish for food | — dogsled<br>— special snowmobiles | — make soapstone carvings<br>— tell stories |

50  Collections 4

# READ AND RESPOND TO TEXT

## Reading Focus

Use a **read and reflect** strategy. Have the students read the article independently, or listen to the audio version as they follow along, to reflect on what "the northern way" means and to find answers to the questions they asked in Get Ready to Read. They might write the answers in their learning logs.

Following the reading, students could
- share their ideas and jottings with a partner or small group.
- assess whether the article answered their questions.
- evaluate whether "The Northern Way" is an appropriate title for the selection, and write a summarizing sentence about what "the northern way" is.

## Reader Response

Students could
- draw a picture showing how the Inuit tracked and hunted caribou in the past and how they track and hunt today.
- write about how the Inuit show respect for animal life.
- contrast the Inuit perspective on hunting with that of the hunters' in "Animal Crimes, Animals Clues."
- read picture books written by the author, Michael Kusugak.

# REVISIT THE TEXT

## Reading

### Find Answers in Text

Prepare questions such as those in the margin for the students to answer. Using the first question as an example, model how to find answers in text. Record some of the strategies you used.

### How to find answers in text

- Read the first sentence of a paragraph to see if it relates to the question.
- Look for sentences that give the answers outright.
- Look for key words in the text that are also in the question.

---

### Get Ready to Read

Ask students to look at the title and the photographs to get a sense of the setting. To help students develop specific purposes for reading, have them read the first few sentences at the beginning of each section and generate questions that they would like answered.

### PICTURE BOOKS BY MICHAEL KUSUGAK

*Baseball Bats for Christmas.* Annick, 1990.

*Hide and Sneak.* Annick, 1992.

*A Promise is a Promise,* co-written with Robert Munsch. Annick, 1989.

### SAMPLE QUESTIONS

- Give two reasons why the Inuit don't depend on food from stores. (p. 47)
- What do the Inuit mean by "living off the land"? (p. 47)
- Name one way in which getting food has become easier for the Inuit. (p. 47)
- How do the Inuit store what they hunt and fish? (p. 48)
- How do Inuit children help provide for their families? (p. 49)

*The Northern Way* 51

Then, invite the students to find the answer to the second question. Ask what strategies they used and add new ones to the list. Students can work in pairs to answer the rest of the questions in their learning logs. Encourage them to talk about strategies they found especially helpful when locating information.

**Assessment** See **Assess Learning**, page 55.

## Writing

### Write a Group Report

*Learning Strategy Card 32*

Use Learning Strategy Card 32 to guide students in writing a report about the caribou. Invite pairs to reread parts of the article that tell about the caribou and to make brief notes. Have them categorize the points and decide on headings for their information.

In the larger group, ask students what headings they used and what points they listed under each one. Record their ideas on the board or on chart paper. Then, ask students what other information they would include in a report on the caribou. Jot down these points, and questions that students would like to answer, under the appropriate headings.

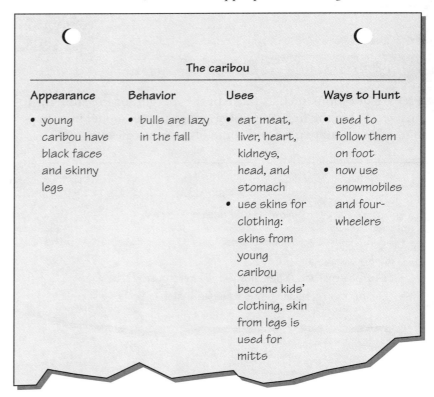

| The caribou | | | |
|---|---|---|---|
| **Appearance** | **Behavior** | **Uses** | **Ways to Hunt** |
| • young caribou have black faces and skinny legs | • bulls are lazy in the fall | • eat meat, liver, heart, kidneys, head, and stomach<br>• use skins for clothing: skins from young caribou become kids' clothing, skin from legs is used for mitts | • used to follow them on foot<br>• now use snowmobiles and four-wheelers |

52  *Collections 4*

Groups of students could each choose one category of questions to research. They might gather information from magazines, books, photo sets with accompanying text, CD-ROMs, and other print and non-print resources. Encourage students to use the Skim and Post-It strategy, described on Learning Strategy Card 28, where appropriate.

Students can write a paragraph about what they learned. (See *Writing a Paragraph*, Learning Strategy Card 31, for a model.) They might share their work with the other groups and invite suggestions for changes. Students could then finish the final draft of their report, possibly including illustrations. Encourage them to compile their reports in a logical order to make a class big book or reference book.

Group members can assume various responsibilities in the editing and revising process, checking their report for
- content, to ensure that information is accurate and presented logically.
- language, to ensure that it is clear and understandable.
- spelling, punctuation, and neatness, so that the report is easy to read.

## Language Workshop — Spelling

• gh pattern; -ful ending; superlatives

*Blackline Master 23*

### Explore and Discover

You can use Blackline Master 23 and the sort, share, discuss, and chart procedure outlined on page 16 to work with the words.

Use words from "Animal Crimes, Animal Clues," as well as those in "The Northern Way," to help students generalize where the "gh," "ph," and "ff" patterns appear in words.

Follow this exploration with a **pretest, study and practise,** and a **post test** as outlined on page 16.

### Study and Practise

Students could
- use Learning Strategy Card 3 as a guide for studying words identified after the pretest.
- spell their more difficult study words on graph paper, shading in squares to form the letters. They can shade patterns or tricky spots in a different color.

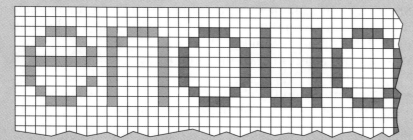

- write each superlative from the list, circle the ending, then write the root word beside it.
- write sentences about the North using their study words, underlining the words they used.

### THE NORTHERN WAY

• gh pattern; -ful ending; superlatives

| useful | enough |
| tough | careful |
| toughest | softest |
| biggest | warmest |
| rough | easiest |
| beautiful | laugh |

#### Theme/Challenge Words

• northern words

| Inuit | caribou |
| snowmobiles | permafrost |
| ptarmigan | |

#### Early Words

• z patterns

| froze | zero | prize |
| these | use | |

*The Northern Way* 53

The nine animals are caribou, foxes, wolverines, polar bears, walrus, whales, seals, Arctic char, and lake trout.

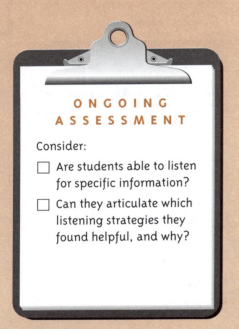

### ONGOING ASSESSMENT

Consider:
- ☐ Are students able to listen for specific information?
- ☐ Can they articulate which listening strategies they found helpful, and why?

## Oral Communication
### Listen for Details

Read aloud the paragraph on page 48, "Though many caribou…through the ice." Have students listen for the names of nine different animals, including two types of fish. They could put out one finger each time they hear an animal mentioned. Then, have students listen a second time, this time only for those animals that provide food.

Read, or have pairs of students read to each other, other sections of text as students listen for and record specific information. Encourage them to talk about strategies that helped them focus on specific details as they listened.

**Other Listening Passages**

| Read… | Listen for details about… |
|---|---|
| • page 46, "We are Inuit…with very short roots will grow." | • the geography of the far north. |
| • page 47, "Maybe you wonder… to follow the caribou." | • how caribou hunting is different than it used to be. |
| • pages 48–49, "Caribou are good…if we do." | • how the Inuit use caribou. |
| • page 49, "What do we do…that is the northern way." | • children and hunting. |

## LINK TO CURRICULUM

### The Arts
### Make an Animal Print

Show students examples of Inuit prints in art books. Invite them to create their own print of an animal that the Inuit use for food or clothing. Students could
- use a blunt object to draw the outline of an animal on a styrofoam plate.
- roll printers ink on the plate.
- turn the plate onto a sheet of paper and press carefully.

Encourage students to mount and display their prints on a bulletin board, or use them as covers for their group reports about the caribou.

54  Collections 4

## Science

### Write an Animal Profile

Have groups of students research and write profiles about animals mentioned in "The Northern Way," using the headings from "Animal Profiles" (*Fur, Feathers, Scales, and Skin*, p. 4) as a guide. Alternatively, students might write reports about northern animals, using Learning Strategy Card 32 as a guide. They could compile their work in a class book and add it to their library or loan it to another class.

## Language Arts

### Create a Glossary

Students may wish to make a glossary of words related to the Inuit and to the animals of the north. (See the Learning Strategy Card *Using a Glossary* for a model.) They might first review the purpose and organization of a glossary. Then, they could list words and find and write definitions, perhaps adding illustrations. Suggest to the students that they may be able to find or deduce the meanings of the words from the text itself.

Students could arrange the words in alphabetical order, then create a glossary bookmark with their words and definitions. They might insert the bookmark in the anthology, at the end of "The Northern Way."

### Read About the Inuit

*Blackline Master 13*

Students may wish to read picture books, information books, or poems that tell about Inuit culture and lifestyle, including "Musk Oxen" on Blackline Master 13. They could meet in groups to discuss the selections and to share what they learned about the Inuit from both the text and illustrations.

A mini-lesson on glossaries was developed in "The Whispering Cloth" in *And the Message Is...* .

**BOOKS ABOUT THE INUIT**

*The Arctic Land*. Bobbie Kalman. Crabtree, 1988.

*Houses of Snow, Skin and Bones*. Bonnie Shemie. Tundra, 1993.

*Journey to the Top of the World*. Janet Foster. Greey de Pencier, 1987.

*A Northern Alphabet*. Ted Harrison. Tundra, 1989.

## Assess Learning

### Reading (see p. 51)

Ask pairs of students to provide, as a **work sample**, their response to a question of their choice. Assess their ability to interpret and answer the question, as well as the appropriateness of the strategy they used to get the answer. Each pair could also write a **reflective comment** on the usefulness of the strategy in this and other situations.

# THEME: PEOPLE'S INTERACTIONS WITH WILD ANIMALS

**Anthology, pages 50–51**

**Ernest Thompson Seton** — *a biography*

**Mary Gauthier** — *an essay*

**Naomi's Geese** — *a book review*

## STUDENT WRITING

## LINK TO THE THEME

After reading the selections, students could
- read other books, including biographies, about people's interactions with animals.
- create a display of books or pictures by Ernest Thompson Seton and other wildlife artists.

## LINK TO THE WRITING PROCESS

### Write a Book Review

*Learning Strategy Card 33*

Using *Book Review*, Learning Strategy Card 33, students could read "Naomi's Geese" to see what features of a review it includes. They might compare this with book reviews in magazines, newspapers, and on-line services. Then, students can write a review for a book they read in the Link to the Theme.

### Language Workshop — Usage

- choose words that are most effective for their purpose (words that identify time)

*Blackline Master 14*

#### Teach/Explore/Discover

Have students identify temporal markers, using sentences from "Naomi's Geese." Then, invite students to suggest other words and phrases that tell about time, and record them on a chart.

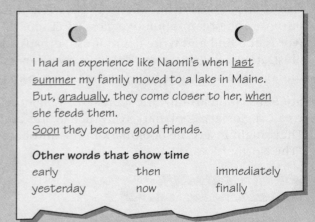

I had an experience like Naomi's when <u>last summer</u> my family moved to a lake in Maine. But, <u>gradually</u>, they come closer to her, <u>when</u> she feeds them.
<u>Soon</u> they become good friends.

**Other words that show time**

| early | then | immediately |
|---|---|---|
| yesterday | now | finally |

#### Practise/Apply

Students could
- complete *Words That Show Time*, Blackline Master 14.
- add to the chart other temporal markers they find in their reading and writing.

### Link to the Writer

Have students reread what Ryan Arseneau said about Mary Gauthier's talk at his school and his visit to Daley Point. Invite them to tell a partner about something they first read or heard about and later experienced first hand, comparing what they imagined things would be like with what they actually saw.

56  *Collections 4*

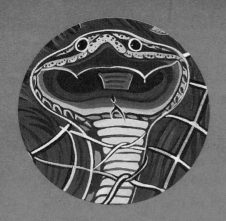

# The Puff Adder Who Was Stuck

In Jackie Lewis's picture book story, a family overcomes its fear of snakes as it struggles to free a puff adder stuck in a wire fence.

Anthology, pages 52–56
Blackline Master 24

## Learning Choices

**LINK TO EXPERIENCE**

Write About Feelings Toward Snakes

Connect with Snake Words

**READ AND RESPOND TO TEXT**

READING FOCUS
- identify and describe elements of stories
- STRATEGY: read and connect

**REVISIT THE TEXT**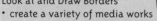

READING
Find Factual Information
- read a variety of fiction and non-fiction materials for different purposes

WRITING
Write a Sequel
- produce pieces of writing using a variety of specific forms
Language Workshop — Spelling
- soft g pattern; en pattern; -al ending (əl)

VISUAL COMMUNICATION
Look at and Draw Borders
- create a variety of media works

**LINK TO CURRICULUM**

LANGUAGE ARTS
Expand Vocabulary

SCIENCE
Research Snakes

THE ARTS
Pantomime a Scene

### Key Learning Expectations

Students will
- identify and describe elements of stories (characters) **(Reading Focus, p. 58)**
- read a variety of fiction and non-fiction materials for different purposes **(Reading Mini Lesson, p. 58)**
- produce pieces of writing using a variety of specific forms (sequel) **(Writing Mini Lesson, p. 59)**
- create a variety of media works (borders) **(Visual Communication Mini Lesson, p. 60)**

## LINK TO EXPERIENCE

### Write About Feelings Toward Snakes

Students could write in their journals how they feel about snakes, and why. They might read their entries to a partner or small group and talk about their experiences.

### Connect with Snake Words

Write words, such as the ones in the chart below, on word cards or chart paper. Invite students to talk about how the words might relate to snakes. You could sort the words as shown.

| Feelings and reactions toward snakes | | Information about snakes | |
|---|---|---|---|
| petrified | scared | creature | gigantic |
| nervous | frantic | poisonous | fluorescent |
| frightened | commotion | dangerous | smooth |
| excitement | | harmless | cobra |
| | | garter snake | hissing |
| | | puff adder | |

Encourage students to suggest other words for the chart. They might use these words in sentences about snakes, play word games, or post the words for reference as they read the story.

*The Puff Adder Who Was Stuck* 57

### Get Ready to Read

Have students read the title and scan the illustrations to predict what this story might be about. If necessary, clarify that the puff adder is a type of snake. Ask students to predict how and where the snake might be stuck, and read to confirm their predictions.

 The homework project for Week 3 is to conduct a survey. See *Home Connections Newsletter*, Blackline Master 2.

# READ AND RESPOND TO TEXT

### Reading Focus

Using a **read and connect** strategy, students could read the story individually or in pairs. Encourage them to pause at *self-selected* points to relate to the feelings and actions of the characters.

If students require guidance, you could suggest that they pause after each of the following points and imagine how they would feel if they were in the character's position:
- page 53, when Opal first sees the snake: *"… I jump back about a metre."*
- page 53, when Opal realizes that the snake is stuck: *"… he can't come over to bite me."*
- page 54, when Opal's mother tries to free the snake as it pecks at her: *"… pecks at her every time she gets near."*

Students could form groups to compare their reactions and responses, and to talk about whether they confirmed the predictions they made in Get Ready to Read.

### Reader Response

Students could
- hold a conversation about the picture book story, using questions such as the following as a guide:
  – **Did you like the way the story ended?**
  – **Have you ever seen a snake near your home? If so, what kind of snake was it?**
  – **Why might it be good to have snakes in your neighborhood?**
  – **What would you do if a snake bit you?**
- read to a partner parts of the story in which the characters reacted strongly.
- write about what they would have done if they had been one of the characters.
- draw another picture for the story.
- find out more about the Puff Adder.
- act out a scene from the story with a partner.

# REVISIT THE TEXT

### Reading

### Find Factual Information

To help students see how Jackie Lewis included factual information in her picture book story, reread page 56, "After all that excitement…around now." State one or two facts about puff adders and ask students to identify other information.

58  Collections 4

Record the ideas on chart paper or on the board. Then, have students skim the rest of the story to find out more about puff adders. Add their ideas to the chart and talk about how weaving factual information into fiction makes the story more realistic.

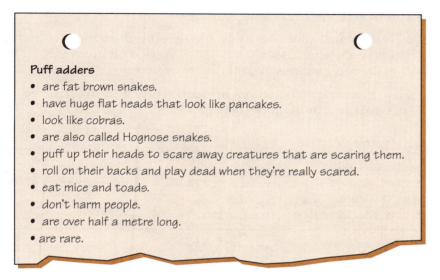

**Puff adders**
- are fat brown snakes.
- have huge flat heads that look like pancakes.
- look like cobras.
- are also called Hognose snakes.
- puff up their heads to scare away creatures that are scaring them.
- roll on their backs and play dead when they're really scared.
- eat mice and toads.
- don't harm people.
- are over half a metre long.
- are rare.

Students might work in small groups to find factual information in the story about other creatures such as cicadas, grass snakes, and garter snakes. They could record their information in new charts and use reference books to confirm what they learned.

## Writing

### Write a Sequel

Talk with students about sequels they've read or seen on TV or in movies. Guide the discussion with questions such as:
- Are there characters in the sequel from the original story?
- Are the stories set in the same place?
- Is the sequel based on an event from the original story?
- Did anything in the sequel not seem right when you compared it with the original?
- Did you prefer the original or the sequel? Why? Why not?

Together, skim "The Puff Adder Who Was Stuck" for details to use in writing a sequel. Jot down where the puff adder lived, what it looked like, how it acted, and what other creatures lived in the area. Then, small groups could write a sequel based on these details. For example, they might tell what happened when the puff adder met the two garter snakes living under the porch.

Encourage students to reread their story to see which elements of the original tale they incorporated in their writing, and to make any necessary changes. Students might add an illustration and display their story on the bulletin board. Or, they might share their story in an Author's Chair. (See *Author's Chair*, Learning Strategy Card 17, for a model.)

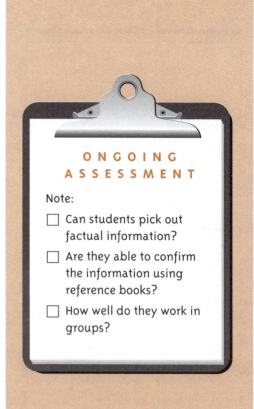

**ONGOING ASSESSMENT**

Note:
- ☐ Can students pick out factual information?
- ☐ Are they able to confirm the information using reference books?
- ☐ How well do they work in groups?

*The Puff Adder Who Was Stuck*

### THE PUFF ADDER WHO WAS STUCK

- soft g pattern; en pattern; -al ending (əl)

| orange | gigantic |
| --- | --- |
| happened | final |
| science | frightened |
| centimetre | endanger |
| enjoy | chicken |
| general | usual |

#### Theme/Challenge Words

- feeling words

| petrified | nervous |
| --- | --- |
| commotion | excitement |
| frantically | |

#### Early Words

- double ending consonants

| off | mitt | yell |
| --- | --- | --- |
| hiss | still | |

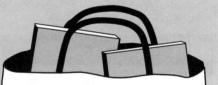

### BOOKS WITH BORDERS

*Chin Chiang and the Dragon's Dance.* Ian Wallace. Douglas & McIntyre, 1984.

*The Honey Hunters.* Francesca Martin. Candlewick, 1992.

*Imagine.* Alison Lester. Houghton Mifflin, 1990.

*Tar Beach.* Faith Ringgold. Crown Books, 1991.

*Town Mouse, Country Mouse.* Jan Brett. G.P. Putnam's Sons, 1994.

*Wildlife ABC.* Jan Thornhill. Greey de Pencier, 1988.

---

## Language Workshop — Spelling

soft g pattern; en pattern; -al ending (əl)

*Blackline Master 24*

### Explore and Discover

You can use Blackline Master 24 and the sort, share, discuss, and chart procedure outlined on page 16 to work with the words. Have students look closely at the words with the "en" pattern.

Follow this exploration with a **pretest, study and practise,** and a **post test** as outlined on page 16.

### Study and Practise

Students could

- use Learning Strategy Card 3 as a guide for studying words identified in the pretest.
- play a tactile game with a partner:

> Give your study cards to your spelling buddy.
>
> Close your eyes.
>
> Have your buddy print each of your words on your forehead with his/her finger.
>
> Guess and spell each word.

- use the eraser end of their pencil to make rubbings of their study words on a colored page from an old magazine.

## Visual Communication

### Look at and Draw Borders

Invite students to look at the illustration on page 53. Focus their attention on the border and ask how it adds to or ties in with the picture and the text. Guide students to notice that the cicadas in each corner show other wildlife in Opal's neighborhood and complement the passage of text that describes the cicadas buzzing in the trees.

Have students look at other drawings with borders in this story and in other picture books. Through discussion, help them see that borders might

- be decorative.
- show something from the text that isn't in the main illustration.
- highlight the colors in the main illustration.
- focus on elements of the main illustration, such as characters or setting.

Encourage students to create another illustration with a border for the story or for their sequel. Alternatively, they might add a border to another piece of art that they have done. Students could use *The Print Shop Deluxe* to create their borders. (See pages 5 and (ii) for more information.)

 See **Assess Learning**, page 61.

# Link to Curriculum

## Language Arts

**Expand Vocabulary**

Students could work in pairs or groups to develop word webs. Some possibilities include words that
- show fear.
- indicate different shades of a color.
- depict animal sounds.

Students might use a dictionary or thesaurus to help them develop their webs.

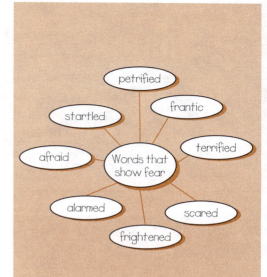

## Science

**Research Snakes**

Students can research different types of snakes, such as garter snakes and grass snakes. They could write a report about what they learned, presenting some facts in text and others in labelled diagrams.

## The Arts

**Pantomime a Scene**

Small groups could pantomime different parts of the story while other groups try to guess which scene is being portrayed. Groups can then present their mimes in sequence, acting out the story from start to finish.

# Assess Learning

## Visual Communication (see p. 60)

Appoint various teams of 4–6 students to **peer-assess** the bordered illustrations. Turn the **criteria** for the borders into questions that can be used for assessment:
- Are the borders decorative?
- Do they show something from the text that is not part of the main illustration?
- Do they highlight colors in the main illustration?
- Do the borders focus on elements of the main illustration, such as characters or setting?

Before submitting their bordered illustrations to the "editorial" panel, each student could do a **self-assessment** of his or her work.

*The Puff Adder Who Was Stuck*

# Digging Up Dinosaurs

In these six newspaper articles, reporters from Canada and Beijing describe exciting dinosaur discoveries.

Anthology, pages 57–61
Blackline Master 24
Learning Strategy Cards 34 and 35

## Learning Choices

**LINK TO EXPERIENCE**

Draw and Tell About a Dinosaur

Make a Dinosaur Display

**READ AND RESPOND TO TEXT**

READING FOCUS
- read a variety of fiction and non-fiction materials for different purposes
- STRATEGY: **narrated reading**

REVISIT THE TEXT

READING
Analyze the Articles
- identify various forms of writing and describe their main characteristics

WRITING
Write a Newspaper Article
- produce pieces of writing using a variety of specific forms

Language Workshop — Spelling
- r-controlled patterns: eer, ear, or, er, and aur; un- prefix

VISUAL COMMUNICATION
Look Closely at a Picture
- analyze media works

**LINK TO CURRICULUM**

LANGUAGE ARTS
Define Paleontology Words

SOCIAL STUDIES
Locate Dinosaur Sites

SCIENCE
Investigate Dinosaur Extinction

THE ARTS
Make a Fossil

## Key Learning Expectations

Students will
- read a variety of fiction and non-fiction materials for different purposes **(Reading Focus, p. 63)**
- identify various forms of writing and describe their main characteristics (media texts) **(Reading Mini Lesson, p. 63)**
- produce pieces of writing using a variety of specific forms (newspaper article) **(Writing Mini Lesson, p. 64)**
- analyze media works (diagrams) **(Visual Communication Mini Lesson, p. 66)**

## LINK TO EXPERIENCE

### Draw and Tell About a Dinosaur

Spark discussion about dinosaurs by reading a poem from *Tyrannosaurus Was a Beast* by Jack Prelutsky (Greenwillow, 1988) or "Dinosaur Dinner" from *Jelly Belly* by Dennis Lee (Macmillan of Canada, 1983). Invite students to brainstorm different kinds of dinosaurs and to tell something interesting about them.

Students could each draw one dinosaur and write a sentence about their choice. They might draw the biggest, smallest, most ferocious, or strangest-looking dinosaur, or the one they like best. Encourage students to use their drawings to make dinosaur picture books to read to younger students.

### Make a Dinosaur Display

Ask students about dinosaur books they've read, movies they've seen, and museum displays they've visited. Encourage them to create their own dinosaur display, including books, pictures, models, newspaper clippings, posters, and so on. Students could write signs or information cards to tell about the items in their display. They might add to the display as they read the articles in "Digging Up Dinosaurs."

62  Collections 4

# Read and Respond to Text

## Reading Focus

Using the **narrated reading** strategy, read aloud the first part of each article to the students, stopping at the points in the chart. Discuss the information together and have students read to the end of the articles on their own or in pairs. One student could read aloud while the other listens for specific information.

| Article | Stopping point | Things to find out |
|---|---|---|
| "Girl finds dinosaur fossil" | "... near Drumheller in southern Alberta." | • Why was Tess's find so important? |
| "Two new dinosaur species found" | "... both found in the desert near Neuquen, Argentina." | • What did Dr. Currie confirm about the new species? |
| "'Jurassic Park' lives!" | "... a variety of gene fragments, it said." | • Why were the contents of the egg important? |
| "Huge T-rex skeleton excites Saskatchewan" | "... he told a news conference." | • What three more details are given about the find? |
| "Dinosaur Diner" | "... long tooth drag marks discovered." | • How do young people help paleontologists in their work? |
| "Alberta badlands discoveries toasted" | "... at the Royal Museum of Paleontology near Drumheller." | • What other dinosaur discoveries were made in Alberta? |

Encourage students to record what they learned in their learning logs. Then, bring students together to discuss the articles.

## Reader Response

Students could
- chart the dinosaur finds mentioned in the articles, telling what was found, by whom, and what the significance was.
- write about the dinosaur find that interested them the most.
-  look in newspapers, in magazines, or on the Internet for other articles about dinosaur finds.
- write a letter to a scientist at the Royal Tyrrell Museum of Paleontology, or another museum, with questions about dinosaurs.
- talk in small groups about words such as "excavate," "imprint," "fossil," "skeletons," "carcass," "site," and "paleontologist" and find their meaning as they relate to dinosaurs.

## Get Ready to Read

Have students read the title and scan the selection to determine that it is written as a series of newspaper articles. Ask them what they know about newspapers—which ones are available in their community, whether they read newspapers, what sections and special features there are, what writing style is used, and so on. Suggest that as students read they think about how each article relates to the title.

Royal Tyrrell Museum of Paleontology
Midland Provincial Park
P.O. Box 7500
Drumheller, Alberta
T0J 0Y0
Telephone: 403-823-7707
Fax: 403-823-7131

*Digging Up Dinosaurs* 63

# REVISIT THE TEXT

## Reading

### Analyze the Articles

Invite the students to skim the articles in "Digging Up Dinosaurs." Ask what they notice about the characteristics of a newspaper article. List their ideas in a chart.

Look closely at one or two articles together. Analyze each article in terms of the characteristics noted. For example, you might point out that the title "Girl finds dinosaur fossil" catches readers' attention because it tells that a young person made an important discovery, and that the title "'Jurassic Park' lives!" makes readers think of the movie. Add to the chart other characteristics that students discover.

Then, have small groups examine another article in "Digging Up Dinosaurs" in terms of its characteristics, and record their observations in a chart. Encourage students to share their findings with other groups.

 To extend the learning, students might analyze articles from local newspapers.

## Writing

### Write a Newspaper Article

*Learning Strategy Card 34*

Using Learning Strategy Card 34, guide students to see how a newspaper article is written. Read aloud the opening sentence or paragraph of an article such as "Two new dinosaur species found." Ask students what questions the sentence or paragraph answers, eliciting that it tells

- *who* made the discovery.
- *what* was discovered.
- *where* it was discovered.

You might read the opening sentences or paragraphs of other articles to show that they often include information about "When?" "Why?" and "How?"

Read the rest of "Two new dinosaur species found" and point out that it provides details, from most important to least important, that support the opening sentence or paragraph. Talk with students about how they could just read the opening sentence or paragraph to find the gist of the article.

---

**ONGOING ASSESSMENT**

Consider:

☐ Are students able to explain how a newspaper article is organized?

☐ Do they incorporate this structure in their own writing?

64  Collections 4

Invite the students to write their own newspaper articles about dinosaur finds they learned about in non-fiction books or documentaries. Or, they might choose a selection from the anthology and turn it into a newspaper article.

 Students could compile their articles in a class newspaper, perhaps using the computer to lay out the design.

### Dinosaur Daily
December 2, 1996

**Scientists revise theories about brachiosaurus**

ANGIERS – Scientists once thought that the brachiosaurus lived in deep lakes, but a recent discovery shows that it probably lived most of its life on land.

### Spirit Special
May 5, 1996

**Dinosaur nesting ground catches scientists' attention**
by Aleksander Khan
*Student Press*

A dinosaur nesting ground, with fossilized nests, eggs, and baby and adult skeletons was recently discovered in the Montana grasslands.

 See **Assess Learning**, page 67.

## Language Workshop — Spelling

- r-controlled patterns: eer, ear, or, er, and aur; un- prefix

*Blackline Master 24*

### Explore and Discover

You can use Blackline Master 24 and the sort, share, discuss, and chart procedure outlined on page 16 to work with the words. Note the two words with the same root word, "uncover" and "discover," and list other words derived from "cover."

Follow this exploration with a **pretest, study and practise,** and a **post test** as outlined on page 16.

### Study and Practise

Students could
- use Learning Strategy Card 3 as a guide for studying words identified in the pretest.
- make word webs with their study cards and print related words or words with the same patterns on cards and add to the web.
- write a short paragraph about a dinosaur dig or museum, using each of their study words at least once and underlining them. They can read their paragraph to a partner, and have the partner dictate the underlined words as a spelling list.

### DIGGING UP DINOSAURS

- r-controlled patterns: eer, ear, or, er, and aur; un- prefix

| | |
|---|---|
| horned | carnivore |
| clearly | deer |
| disappear | uncover |
| unwrap | anymore |
| discover | unusual |
| years | dinosaur |

#### Theme/Challenge Words

- dinosaur words

| | |
|---|---|
| prehistoric | skeletons |
| museum | Tyrannosaurus rex |
| fossilized | |

#### Early Words

- sounds of oo pattern

| | | |
|---|---|---|
| tools | tooth | hoop |
| hook | took | |

*Digging Up Dinosaurs*

## Visual Communication

### Look Closely at a Picture

To help students identify main information and important details in an illustration, show them a picture of a dinosaur scene. Invite them to scan the picture for an overall view, then take away the picture and have them describe in general terms what they saw.

Show students the picture several more times, and suggest that they focus on a different element each time:
- the particular type of dinosaur
- what the dinosaur looks like
- what it's doing
- important details in the background
- minor details in the background

Have students summarize the main idea of the picture and the supporting details, and share their impressions. Encourage them to suggest a title for the illustration.

Students could work in pairs or small groups to view other pictures in the anthology and in other resources, noting the main focus and supporting details.

## Link to Curriculum

### Language Arts

#### Define Paleontology Words

Invite students to create a word bank of paleontology terms. They can define each word, checking its meaning in a dictionary or in other books. Some students may wish to add the words to their personal dictionary. (See *Keeping a Personal Dictionary,* Learning Strategy Card 1, for a model.) Others might use the words to play a word game.

### Social Studies

#### Locate Dinosaur Sites

Students could list all the places mentioned in the article where dinosaur fossils were found, as well as other dinosaur sites they have heard or read about. Encourage them to locate these places on a map.

If there are fossil locations nearby, students may wish to visit them and write in their learning logs about discoveries that have been made there. Or, they could visit local museums or dinosaur exhibits and take notes about what they see.

---

Fossil: animal or plant remains that are preserved in rocks

Triceratops: a plant-eating dinosaur with three horns and a plate covering its neck

## Science

### Investigate Dinosaur Extinction

*Learning Strategy Card 35*

Have students reread the last paragraph of " 'Jurassic Park' Lives!" (page 58). Explain that this is only one theory of dinosaur extinction. Students can read different newspaper articles and non-fiction books to find other theories, or they may suggest theories of their own. They could talk in small groups about which theory seems most feasible, or they might hold an electronic discussion using the Internet. Encourage students to use Learning Strategy Card 35 as a guide.

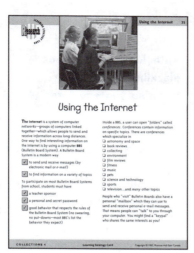

## The Arts

### Make a Fossil

Students could make fossils similar to the one Tess Owen found by
- pressing objects such as leaves or acorns into clay or play dough.
- pouring Plaster of Paris over the clay or play dough.
- peeling away the clay or play dough when the plaster dries.

Encourage students to display their fossils along with a written explanation of the significance of "the discovery."

# Assess Learning

## Writing (see p. 64)

Assess the newspaper article that the students wrote using the **criteria** and **model** on *Newspaper Article*, Learning Strategy Card 34. The example of student writing shown is at the expected level for Grade 4.

---

**Shake Scare**

by Mike Roy

COE HILL — Opal got scared by a snake stuck in a chicken wire fence this morning. She thought it was a cobra and she called her mother right away. Sophie and Danny and Jocy saw the snake too. Sophie tried to kill it. Opal said "no." Opal's mother put a towel over the snake and then she cut the fence so it went under the chicken house.

---

*Digging Up Dinosaurs* **67**

# An Interview with Father Goose

Chris Fox's interview with Bill Lishman reveals why the Canadian naturalist, artist, author, and filmmaker is known as Father Goose.

Anthology, pages 62–65
Blackline Master 25
Learning Strategy Cards 36 and 37

## Learning Choices

**LINK TO EXPERIENCE**

Talk About Interviews
Draw a Trained Animal

**READ AND RESPOND TO TEXT**

READING FOCUS
- identify the main idea in a piece of writing, and provide supporting details
- STRATEGY: **read and reflect**

**REVISIT THE TEXT**

READING
Investigate Vocabulary
- make inferences while reading

WRITING
Write a Business Letter
- produce pieces of writing using a variety of specific forms
Language Workshop — Spelling
- eigh pattern; eight pattern; number words

ORAL COMMUNICATION
Conduct an Interview
- express and respond to ideas and opinions concisely and clearly

**LINK TO CURRICULUM**

LANGUAGE ARTS
Prepare Interview Questions

SCIENCE
Investigate Migration

THE ARTS
Design a Poster

### Key Learning Expectations

Students will
- identify the main idea in a piece of writing, and provide supporting details (**Reading Focus, p. 69**)
- make inferences while reading (**Reading Mini Lesson, p. 69**)
- produce pieces of writing using a variety of specific forms (business letter) (**Writing Mini Lesson, p. 70**)
- express and respond to ideas and opinions concisely and clearly (**Oral Communication Mini Lesson, p. 71**)

## LINK TO EXPERIENCE

### Talk About Interviews

Invite students to brainstorm interviews they've seen, heard, or read, and to talk about what they learned from these interviews. Students could categorize the interviews and create a web on chart paper or on an overhead transparency.

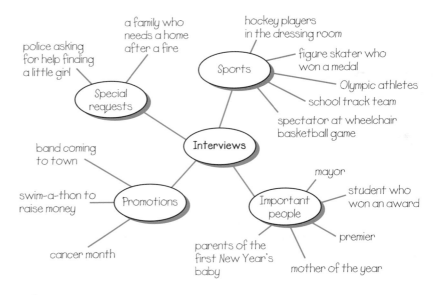

Students might imagine people they would like to interview—family members, people in the community, celebrities—and list questions they would ask.

68  Collections 4

### Draw a Trained Animal

Discuss with students what behaviors humans teach animals to do, and what training is involved. Students could each draw a picture showing an animal performing the behavior and write a short paragraph. They might compile their completed pictures in a class book about animal training.

## READ AND RESPOND TO TEXT

### Reading Focus

Use the **read and reflect** strategy. As students read the interview independently or with a partner, they could reflect on Bill Lishman's responses, perhaps jotting down the key parts of his answers. Bring students together to talk about what they learned from the interview about Bill Lishman and his work.

 Students may wish to listen to the audio version of the interview before reading the selection.

### Reader Response

Students could
- write about something that especially amazed or interested them about Bill Lishman's adventures with geese.
- with a partner, recall the steps that Bill Lishman followed in training the geese, then reread related parts of the interview.
- write a poem about how it would feel to fly with the birds.
- read Bill Lishman's book *Father Goose and His Goslings*.

## REVISIT THE TEXT

### Reading

#### Investigate Vocabulary

*mini* LESSON

Have students skim the selection to find the names of seven different professions. Write their suggestions on the board. Then, focus students' attention on the words "naturalist," "artist," "biologist," and "ornithologist." Point out clues that students could use to determine each word's meaning. For example:
- underline the "-ist" suffix and explain that it indicates someone who does or knows something.
- identify the root word.
- model how to infer a word's meaning using the word origin in a dictionary. ▶

### Get Ready to Read

Have students read the title to discover that the selection is an interview. Then, ask them to read the first question and answer on page 62 to learn who Father Goose is and what the interview will be about.

*An Interview with Father Goose*

Encourage students to suggest other occupational words that end in "-ist." They might skim "Digging Up Dinosaurs" (*Fur, Feathers, Scales, and Skin*, p. 57) for examples. Talk about the words together and add them to the list.

Then, invite students to choose an occupation of interest to them, find out more about it, and write a definition on a word card. They could use these cards as the basis for riddles to ask other students.

As students work with the "-ist" words, they have the opportunity to investigate word derivations and origins, and to read longer words by focusing on shorter parts such as syllables.

> naturalist: a person who studies animals and plants

> artist: a person who draws, paints, or does other creative things

> biologist: a person who studies living things

> ornithologist: a trained person who studies birds

## Writing

### Write a Business Letter

*mini LESSON*

*Learning Strategy Card 36*

Ask students how they could find out more about people or organizations like Operation Migration that are concerned with animals or that help wildlife. Elicit that one possibility is to write a business letter or a letter of inquiry.

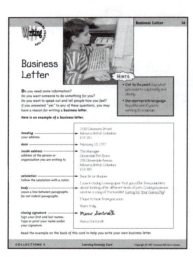

To help students identify the features of a business letter, show them the sample business letter on Learning Strategy Card 36. As you examine the body of the letter, talk about the language style. Compare it with the language style of the friendly letter on Learning Strategy Card 2, eliciting that a business letter is more formal because the writer usually doesn't know the person he or she is writing to.

On their own, in pairs, or in small groups, students could write to different wildlife organizations. Help them establish the purpose of their letter through questioning:
- Do you want to find out more about the person's or organization's work?
- Do you want to find out how you can help preserve wildlife?
- Are you writing to express a concern?

You might suggest that students refer to *The Canadian Almanac + Directory* for the addresses of various environmental and naturalist agencies, including
- The Canadian Nature Federation.
- The World Wildlife Fund.
- The Sierra Club of Canada.

Alternatively, if you have access to the Internet, students could search the World Wide Web for organizations that help wildlife.

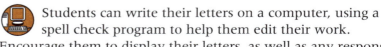

Students can write their letters on a computer, using a spell check program to help them edit their work. Encourage them to display their letters, as well as any responses they receive, on the unit bulletin board.

## Language Workshop — Spelling

• eigh pattern; eight pattern; number words

*Blackline Master 25*

### Explore and Discover

You can use Blackline Master 25 and the sort, share, discuss, and chart procedure outlined on page 16 to work with the words. Group "<u>tw</u>enty," "<u>tw</u>elve," and "<u>tw</u>o" together. Note the hyphens in some of the other number words.

Follow this exploration with a **pretest, study and practise,** and a **post test** as outlined on page 16.

### Study and Practise

Students could
- use Learning Strategy Card 3 as a guide for studying words identified in the pretest.
- softly say the words on their word cards, clap out the syllables, and place the cards in piles according to the number of syllables.
- play a tic-tac-toe game with a partner. The players should make a fairly large game grid and, in turn, each use a different colored marker to write one of their study words in a square.

## Oral Communication

### Conduct an Interview

*Learning Strategy Card 37*

Invite students to reread "Interview with Father Goose" and to think about the interviews they mentioned in the Link to Experience. Ask what made these interviews interesting and informative. Using Learning Strategy Card 37 as a guide, identify points that interviewers should keep in mind before, during, and after the interview.

 Have students work with a partner to plan an interview, perhaps with the person they identified in the Link to Experience. Encourage them to tape-record their interviews to share with the class. Students could talk about what worked well and what they would do differently next time.

 See **Assess Learning**, page 72.

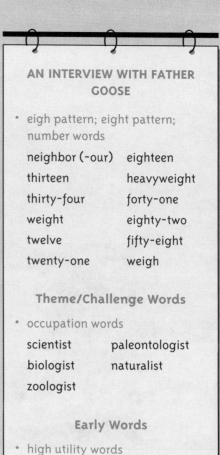

**AN INTERVIEW WITH FATHER GOOSE**

• eigh pattern; eight pattern; number words

| | |
|---|---|
| neighbor (-our) | eighteen |
| thirteen | heavyweight |
| thirty-four | forty-one |
| weight | eighty-two |
| twelve | fifty-eight |
| twenty-one | weigh |

**Theme/Challenge Words**

• occupation words

| | |
|---|---|
| scientist | paleontologist |
| biologist | naturalist |
| zoologist | |

**Early Words**

• high utility words

| | | |
|---|---|---|
| walks | who | two |
| very | think | |

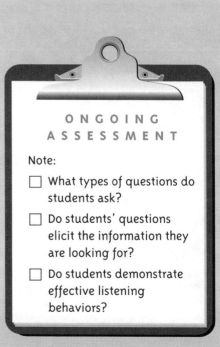

### ONGOING ASSESSMENT

Note:

☐ What types of questions do students ask?

☐ Do students' questions elicit the information they are looking for?

☐ Do students demonstrate effective listening behaviors?

*An Interview with Father Goose*

# Link to Curriculum

## Language Arts

### Prepare Interview Questions

Invite students to reread the article and to jot down questions that they would like to ask Father Goose. These could be questions about his work with geese or about his projects with sandhill cranes, whooping cranes, and trumpeter swans. Students might include their questions in a letter to Bill Lishman.

## Science

### Investigate Migration

Students might work in small groups to find out more about migration. The group members could each research one aspect of the topic and present their findings in an oral report. Or, students might each write a paragraph about what they learned. (See *Writing a Paragraph*, Learning Strategy Card 31, for a model.) They could add illustrations and compile their pages to make a book in the shape of a bird.

## The Arts

### Design a Poster

Encourage students to design a poster to support Operation Wildlife or another wildlife organization. They might use *The Print Shop Deluxe* or other graphics software to design their poster. (See pages 5 and (ii) for more information.) Students could display their posters in the hallway, in the school or public library, or in other community buildings.

# Assess Learning

## Oral Communication (see p. 71)

Students could place a tape-recorded copy of their interviews in their portfolios as a **work sample** demonstrating their ability to conduct an interview.

Encourage students, as well, to do a **self-assessment** of their interviewing experiences, using prompts such as:
- What I learned about interviewing
- What I did well in the interview
- What I would change next time I do an interview

72    Collections 4

# THEME: PEOPLE'S INTERACTIONS WITH WILD ANIMALS

**Anthology, pages 66–67**

> **Letters from Endangered Animals** — *letters*
>
> **Piping Plover** — *a memoir*

## LINK TO THE THEME

After reading the selections, students could

- find out about endangered species in their community.
- make a collage of endangered animals.

## LINK TO THE WRITING PROCESS

### Write a Letter

Students might choose an animal and write, from the animal's point of view, about why it is endangered. They could use the pattern of writing in "Letters from Endangered Animals." Students might display their letters along with the collages they created in the Link to the Theme.

### Language Workshop — Grammar

- use verb tenses correctly and appropriately (past tense)

*Blackline Master 15*

### Teach/Explore/Discover

To help students recognize the past tense of verbs, write the following sentences from "Piping Plover" on the board or on an overhead transparency.
- She <u>fixed</u> up its wing.
- When I <u>looked</u> at it closer, I <u>discovered</u> that it was a bird.
- It <u>jumped</u> on the ground and <u>flapped</u> its wing.
- It flew up and <u>circled</u> over us a few times.

Ask students what they know about the underlined words. Elicit that the verbs tell about something that happened in the past. Write the present tense of each verb beside the past tense and identify different ways to form the past tense: adding "-d," adding "-ed," and doubling the final consonant before adding "-ed." List the verbs in a chart, under the appropriate category.

Invite students to point out other verbs in these sentences. As they mention "was" and "flew," talk about the fact that these verbs don't follow the regular pattern for forming the past tense. Add these verbs to the chart, under a fourth category.

| Add -d | Add -ed |
|---|---|
| circle-circled | fix-fixed |
|  | look-looked |
|  | discover-discovered |
|  | jump-jumped |

| Double the final consonant, then add -ed | Irregular |
|---|---|
| flap-flapped | is-was |
|  | fly-flew |

### Practise/Apply

Students could
- complete *Verbs in the Past*, Blackline Master 15.
- identify whether other verbs in "Piping Plover" are in the past or present tense, explaining how they know.

### Link to the Writer

Daniel says that sometimes expressing yourself in writing can be even better than expressing yourself through speech. Encourage students to think of other ways they express themselves, for example, through art, drama, or dance. Students might talk about which means of expression they prefer.

*Student Writing* 73

# You Asked About Pets

This selection from *Owl* magazine includes students' questions about pets along with answers that are sometimes surprising.

Anthology, pages 68–71
Blackline Masters 16 and 25

## Learning Choices

**LINK TO EXPERIENCE**

Write About Pets

Brainstorm Questions About Pets

**READ AND RESPOND TO TEXT**

READING FOCUS
- read a variety of fiction and non-fiction materials for different purposes
- STRATEGY: **double look**

REVISIT THE TEXT

READING
Identify Synonyms and Antonyms
- identify synonyms and antonyms for familiar words

WRITING
Experiment with Typography
- produce pieces of writing using a variety of specific forms
Language Workshop — Spelling
- er pattern; -ly ending; compound words

VISUAL COMMUNICATION
View Animals in Art
- analyze media works

**LINK TO CURRICULUM**

LANGUAGE ARTS
Read Stories About Pets

SCIENCE
Research Pets

THE ARTS
Make a 3-D Pet Card

## Key Learning Expectations

Students will
- read a variety of fiction and non-fiction materials for different purposes (**Reading Focus, p. 75**)
- identify synonyms and antonyms for familiar words (**Reading Mini Lesson, p. 75**)
- produce pieces of writing using a variety of specific forms (**Writing Mini Lesson, p. 76**)
- analyze media works (pictures) (**Visual Communication Mini Lesson, p. 77**)

## LINK TO EXPERIENCE

### Write About Pets

Invite students to take a few moments to reflect on pets. They could write in their journals about some of their thoughts, memories, or wishes. Some students may choose to share their journal entries with one another while others may prefer to keep their writing private.

### Brainstorm Questions About Pets

Invite students to think of as many different types of pets as they can. Note their ideas on the board. Then, have students work in small groups to brainstorm interesting questions about the pets, recording their questions on strips of paper.

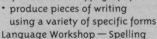 Bring the groups together to sort the questions, then display them in the inquiry area. Students can bring books, magazines, and other materials from home to help them answer the questions.

> Why do snakes shed their skin?

> Are cats right-pawed or left-pawed?

> Why do parrots talk?

74  Collections 4

# READ AND RESPOND TO TEXT

## Reading Focus

Use a **double look** strategy. Students can work in pairs to first read the questions in the selection and to think of possible answers. Then, they could read the answers and find out whether their hypotheses were correct.

If necessary, model the strategy with the whole class before breaking into pairs, using the questions and answers on page 68 of the anthology. When the students finish reading, bring the class together to talk about the selection.

## Reader Response

Students could
- hold a conversation about the selection, using the following questions as a guide:
  - **Did you like the selection? Why? Why not?**
  - **Have you ever wondered about any of the questions in the text? Which one(s)?**
  - **Did any answers surprise you? Which one(s)?**
- role-play some answers, speaking as if they were the pets.
- write in their literature response journals about how the answers in the text compare with what they've always thought.
- find out more about one of the pets in the selection.

# REVISIT THE TEXT

## Reading

### Identify Synonyms and Antonyms

Write a sentence such as the following on the board: "Your cat sniffs, (opens) its mouth, and (traps) the odor on its tongue" (page 68). Focus first on the underlined words, asking students to generate synonyms, or words that mean the same. Then, ask them to give antonyms, or opposites, for the circled words. Have students read the sentence with the synonyms, then with the antonyms.

Encourage students to work in pairs or small groups to find words such as those in the margin in context. Have students suggest a synonym, an antonym, or both if possible, for each word.

To extend the learning, students might write synonyms or antonyms on word cards, then use the cards to play a game such as Concentration.

See **Assess Learning**, page 78.

---

### Get Ready to Read

Have students examine the title, illustrations, and format of the selection. Ask where they have seen a question and answer format before.

The homework project for Week 4 is to make a 3-D animal. See *Home Connections Newsletter*, Blackline Master 2.

Find synonyms for...
- rodent
- swine
- odor
- traps
- feline/cat/kitty
- inserted
- unique

Find antonyms for...
- lost
- found
- difficult
- external
- protect
- dead
- opens
- traps

*You Asked About Pets* 75

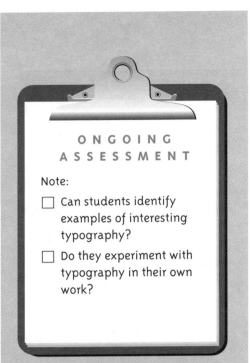

## Writing

### Experiment with Typography

To encourage students to experiment with typography in the publishing/sharing phase of the writing process, focus their attention on the headings in the selection. Guide them to notice the type of face, the way the words are displayed, and the use of different colors.

Students could examine other selections in *Fur, Feathers, Scales, and Skin* for more examples of interesting typography. For example, they might notice
- the way COLLECTIONS is printed on the cover.
- the use of boldface for the categories in "Animal Profiles" (p. 4).
- the lettering in the title of "Desert Tortoise" (p. 12) and "Lily Pad Pond" (p. 14).

Talk with students about the effect of using interesting typography.

 Suggest that students choose a piece of writing that they would like to share and focus on one or two elements of typography. If students have access to a computer, they could experiment with different fonts. Other students may wish to experiment with colored pencils or pens in their work.

## ONGOING ASSESSMENT

Note:
☐ Can students identify examples of interesting typography?
☐ Do they experiment with typography in their own work?

### Language Workshop — Spelling

• er pattern; -ly ending; compound words

*Blackline Master 25*

#### Explore and Discover

You can use Blackline Master 25 and the sort, share, discuss, and chart procedure outlined on page 16 to work with the words.

Determine the root word for words with endings, and select a few for a web of derivatives.

Follow this exploration with a **pretest**, **study and practise**, and a **post test** as outlined on page 16.

#### Study and Practise

Students could
- use Learning Strategy Card 3 as a guide for studying words identified after the pretest.
- indicate syllable breaks for each word by drawing a curved line under the letters that go together to make a syllable. They can work with a partner to clap rhythmically as they spell the words in syllables.
- print their study words along a line that they have drawn.

---

### YOU ASKED ABOUT PETS

• er pattern; -ly ending; compound words

| | |
|---|---|
| toothbrush | usually |
| normally | happily |
| leftovers | easily |
| shelter | computer |
| goldfish | covering |
| overcrowding | probably |

#### Theme/Challenge Words

• pet words

| | |
|---|---|
| veterinarian | gene |
| aquarium | behavior (-our) |
| gerbils | |

#### Early Words

• oo and ou patterns

| | | |
|---|---|---|
| could | would | should |
| good | look | |

## Visual Communication

**View Animals in Art**

Invite students to look at the picture of the cat on page 68 and to compare it with the picture of the cat on page 77. Alternatively, they might view the picture of the rabbit on page 71 and compare it with the picture of the rabbit on page 78. Ask students which artistic style they prefer, and why.

Have students find other pictures of cats or rabbits, perhaps in books in the inquiry area. Or, they might look at how another animal is depicted in various illustrations. Students can create a display showing different artistic styles and write a note about what makes a particular style interesting or unique.

Students may wish to draw their own animal picture and add it to the display with a note about the style that they chose.

# LINK TO CURRICULUM

## Language Arts

**Read Stories About Pets**

Invite students to read fictional stories about people and their pets. Small groups could talk about the variety of pets—both common and uncommon—that they encountered. Students who read about the same kind of pet might compare how they were portrayed, reading humorous or touching passages to one another.

## Science

**Research Pets**

Students may wish to research the questions about pets that they wrote on sentence strips in the Link to Experience. Encourage them to use print and non-print resources to answer the questions. For example, students might talk with people they know who are veterinarians or who work in pet stores.

Have students write the answers to their questions on the back of the sentence strips and post them in the inquiry area.

As an alternative to the sentence strips, students might set up a computer data base where they use one field to show the questions and another to show the answers.

**BOOKS ABOUT PETS**

*Courtney*. John Burningham. Crown Books, 1994.

*Harry's Mad*. Dick King-Smith. Puffin, 1984.

*Owls in the Family*. Farley Mowat. McClelland & Stewart, 1961.

*Paddington* series. Michael Bond. Houghton Mifflin.

*Ralph S. Mouse*. Beverly Cleary. Dell, 1982.

*You Asked About Pets*

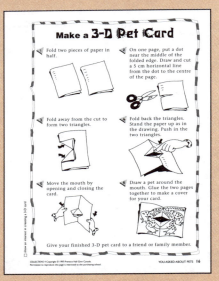

Blackline Master 16

## The Arts

### Make a 3-D Pet Card

*Blackline Master 16*

Students can follow the instructions on Blackline Master 16 to create a three-dimensional pet card with a mouth that opens and closes. They could give their card to a friend or family member on a special occasion.

 **Assess Learning**

### Reading (see p. 75)

Focus on five or six students as they work on the synonym and antonym activity related to the anthology or play the Concentration game. Make an **anecodotal comment** in your record book about whether
- students understand what synonyms and antonyms are.
- they are able to contribute additional synonyms or antonyms.

For students who might benefit from reteaching or more experience with the concept, you may wish to partner them with students who have demonstrated ability to do the task. In these paired groupings, the student teacher can repeat the strategy used in the lesson by applying it to a new story or to a piece of student writing, or students can play another game of Concentration.

78  Collections 4

# Keeping Old Friends

In this short story by Chris Halvorson, a family brings a new puppy into its home when it realizes that its 13-year-old dog, Holly, will not live much longer.

Anthology, pages 72–75
Blackline Masters 17, 18, 19, and 26

## Learning Choices

### LINK TO EXPERIENCE
Make a Pet Scrapbook
Tell About the Loss of a Pet

### READ AND RESPOND TO TEXT

**READING FOCUS**
- read a variety of fiction and non-fiction materials for different purposes
- STRATEGY: **read and reflect**

### REVISIT THE TEXT

**READING**
Compare Ideas in a Story and Poem
- develop their opinions by reading a variety of materials

**WRITING**
Language Workshop — Style
- use correctly the conventions of punctuation
Language Workshop — Spelling
- different ending patterns

**ORAL COMMUNICATION**
Discuss Pet Problems and Solutions
- demonstrate the ability to concentrate by identifying main points and staying on topic

### LINK TO CURRICULUM

**LANGUAGE ARTS**
Draw a Cartoon Strip

**SCIENCE**
Research Dogs

**THE ARTS**
Role-Play Consoling a Friend
Make a Line Drawing

## Key Learning Expectations

Students will
- read a variety of fiction and non-fiction materials for different purposes **(Reading Focus, p. 80)**
- develop their opinions by reading a variety of materials **(Reading Mini Lesson, p. 80)**
- use correctly the conventions of punctuation (contractions) **(Writing Mini Lesson, p. 81)**
- demonstrate the ability to concentrate by identifying main points and staying on topic **(Oral Communication Mini Lesson, p. 82)**

## LINK TO EXPERIENCE

### Make a Pet Scrapbook

 Invite students to draw a picture of a special or funny moment they've had with a pet. If students have never had a pet, they might talk with friends or family members about their special memories. They could show in their drawings what the pet looked like at the time and write a caption to tell what was happening. Students may wish to make their picture look like a photograph by drawing on a photograph-sized piece of paper or by adding a border. Students can paste their "photos" on a larger sheet of paper, and compile their pages to make a classroom pet scrapbook.

### Tell About the Loss of a Pet

Students could meet in small groups to talk about the loss of a pet. They might describe what happened, how they and others felt at the time, and how they dealt with the loss. Some students may wish to share their experiences through drama, perhaps presenting a mime or puppet play.

*Keeping Old Friends*

## Get Ready to Read

Initiate a discussion about friendship, asking students how they feel about their old and new friends. Then, have students read the title, scan the illustrations, and predict what the story will be about and what the title might mean. They can read to verify their predictions.

# Read and Respond to Text

## Reading Focus

*Blackline Master 17*

 Use the **read and reflect** strategy. Students might read the story or listen to the audio version independently or in pairs. They could stop at the points indicated on *Read and Reflect Grid for Keeping Old Friends*, Blackline Master 17, to reflect on what was happening at the time and how the characters were feeling. They can complete the grid, then compare their responses with a small group.

## Reader Response

Students could
- hold a conversation about the story, using questions such as the following as a guide:
  - **Is this a happy story? a sad story? both?**
  - **When did you first suspect that Holly might die? What clues did the author put in the story to prepare you for, or foreshadow, the ending?**
  - **Do you like the way the story ended?**
  - **What would you have done had you been a member of the family in the story?**
- write in their literature response journals about a personal experience that came to mind as they read the story.
- use the description of Holly, as well as what they know about Airedale dogs, to draw Holly doing something she enjoyed.
- read to a partner a part of the story that they found especially touching.

 See **Assess Learning**, page 84.

# Revisit the Text

## Reading

### Compare Ideas in a Story and Poem

*mini LESSON*

Blackline Master 18

*Blackline Master 18*

Prepare Blackline Master 18 as an overhead transparency and/or duplicate copies for each student. Read the poem as the students follow along. Ask students about their impressions of the poem. Then, read the poem again, this time having the students focus on how "The Accident" is similar to and different from "Keeping Old Friends."

80  Collections 4

The students could work in pairs to create a Venn diagram showing the similarities and differences. Ask the pairs to share their ideas and together develop a collaborative diagram on the board or on an overhead transparency. You might encourage each pair to add a point to the diagram.

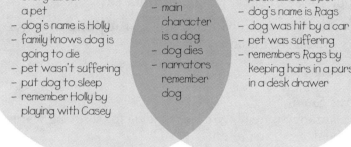

Help the students realize that authors can use different forms to focus on the same ideas. To apply their learning, students can compare another poem or story about a pet dying with "Keeping Old Friends."

## Writing

### Language Workshop — Style

*Blackline Master 19*

Write on the board "Let's see what she's going to bring us now" (p. 72). Circle "Let's" and explain that this is another way to say "Let us," emphasizing that the apostrophe replaces the letter "u." Repeat the process for "she's." Elicit that contractions create a friendlier, less formal tone by having students read the sentences with and without the contractions.

To apply this, have the students complete Blackline Master 19. As they identify the two words that form each contraction in questions 1–8, they should realize that sometimes the apostrophe replaces more than one letter.

To extend their learning, students might look for contractions in another selection in *Fur, Feathers, Scales, and Skin* or in another book that they are reading. To keep the activity meaningful and focused, provide a ten-minute time limit. Then, students could meet with a partner to talk about the contractions they noticed and how they were formed.

**BOOKS ABOUT LOSING PETS**

*The Accident.* Carol Carrick. Houghton Mifflin, 1981.

*Bonesy and Isabel.* Michael Rosen. Harcourt Brace, 1995.

*The Tenth Good Thing About Barney.* Judith Viorst. Simon & Schuster Children's, 1971.

Blackline Master 19

*Keeping Old Friends*

### KEEPING OLD FRIENDS

- different ending patterns

  | carried | changes |
  |---|---|
  | clapping | children |
  | laughing | carrying |
  | noticed | putting |
  | paddling | neighbors (-ours) |
  | puppies | saying |

  **Theme/Challenge Words**

- dog words

  | retriever | Airedale |
  |---|---|

  students' choices of other breeds of dogs

  **Early Words**

- -ed ending

  | walked | helped | jumped |
  |---|---|---|
  | sailed | rolled | |

## Language Workshop — Spelling
• different ending patterns

*Blackline Master 26*

### Explore and Discover

You can use Blackline Master 26 and the sort, share, discuss, and chart procedure outlined on page 16 to work with the words.

With students, identify the root word for each word. Draw attention to the irregular plural for "children."

Follow this exploration with a **pretest, study and practise,** and a **post test** as outlined on page 16.

### Study and Practise

Students could
- use Learning Strategy Card 3 as a guide for studying words identified after the pretest.
- sort their study cards according to endings and write the words from each grouping on a chart showing ways to add endings.

| double letter | y to i | silent e | no change | other |
|---|---|---|---|---|
| clapping | puppies | noticed | laughing | children |
| putting | carried | changes | neighbors | |
| | | paddling | carrying | |
| | | | saying | |

- write tongue twisters based on their study words. They can write the spelling words with a colored marker for emphasis. Students could give their tongue twisters to a partner to read.

> New **neighbors** never **noticed** Nellie.

## Oral Communication

### Discuss Pet Problems and Solutions

Recall the way the family dealt with the problem of a dying pet. Pose several problems related to pets, and invite students to suggest others:
- Your pet is very old.
- Your dog bit your neighbor.

- A friend gives you a kitten that you know your parents won't let you keep.
- A stray dog is roaming around the schoolyard.
- It's your responsibility to take care of your new pet.

Arrange students in groups of three according to the problem they would like to solve. Provide a time frame of about ten minutes and have each group brainstorm and record several possible solutions, then choose the solution that they think is best.

> If a stray dog is roaming around the schoolyard, we could
> - tell the teacher on yard duty.
> - check to see whether the dog is wearing a collar.
> - ask around to see if anyone's noticed a Dog Lost poster.
> - call the Humane Society to see if someone's reported a missing dog.

Each group can present its solution to the rest of the class and explain its reasoning. Students might invite feedback from their classmates about the appropriateness of their solutions.

## INK TO CURRICULUM

### Language Arts

**Draw a Cartoon Strip**

Invite students to draw a cartoon strip telling about an adventure with a pet, perhaps adapting part of "Keeping Old Friends" as a cartoon format. Students could use both speech and thought balloons to help readers know what the characters are thinking and feeling. They can read their cartoons to younger students in the school or post them in the hallway for others to enjoy.

### Science

**Research Dogs**

Refer students to the part of the story that describes Airedale dogs (p. 72). Have them brainstorm other breeds of dogs. Then, pairs could choose one breed to research, perhaps using the Skim and Post-It strategy to gather information from print materials. (See *Skim and Post-It*, Learning Strategy Card 28, for a model.)

Students could present what they learned on a class chart with illustrations and interesting facts organized in headings or as answers to questions.

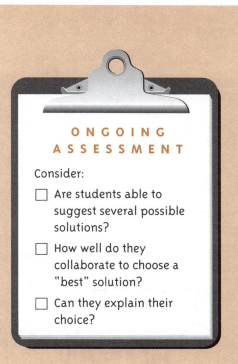

**ONGOING ASSESSMENT**

Consider:
- [ ] Are students able to suggest several possible solutions?
- [ ] How well do they collaborate to choose a "best" solution?
- [ ] Can they explain their choice?

Some students may prefer to find out about police dogs, hearing ear dogs, or seeing eye dogs.

*Keeping Old Friends*

## The Arts

### Role-Play Consoling a Friend

Invite students to role-play a scene where one student is a child whose dog has died and the other is a friend who offers consolation. As students practise their scene, they could think about
- what tone of voice they will use.
- how their words might make their friend feel.
- whether there might be a kinder way to say what they want to say.
- what words of consolation would help them if their dog died.

At the end of the role play, encourage students to talk about how the dramatization helped them understand how someone who has lost a pet feels.

### Make a Line Drawing

Invite students to draw a picture of a pet, using very short, continuously drawn pencil lines to create a sense of furriness. They might experiment with different types of line strokes to add background to the scene. Students could create a bulletin board display of their black and white sketches mounted on black paper.

## Assess Learning

### Reader Response (see p. 80)

Plan time to assess the response activity that the students chose. To prepare for the assessment, students could complete a **self-assessment** using a *Reader Response Activity Master* from the COLLECTIONS 4 Assessment Handbook.

Alternatively, you might prefer to ask all the students to write answers to the questions in "hold a conversation about the story." Use the written answers as a **work sample** assignment or test of how well students comprehend a story.

Place the students' answers and your marking in the portfolios. Focus your marking on how well the students are able to provide proofs for their opinions.

**Note**: With some students, you may prefer to hold individual conferences so that they can answer orally.

# Pet Poems

Five poets use rhyme, rhythm, and imagery to tell about pets.

Anthology, pages 76–78
Learning Strategy Card 38

## Learning Choices

**LINK TO EXPERIENCE**

Read Poems About Pets

Make Pet Word Webs

**READ AND RESPOND TO TEXT**

READING FOCUS
- read a variety of fiction and non-fiction materials for different purposes
- STRATEGY: listen and visualize

REVISIT THE TEXT

READING
Identify Poetic Techniques
- state their own interpretation of a written work, using evidence from the work and from their own knowledge and experience

WRITING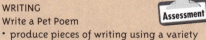
Write a Pet Poem
- produce pieces of writing using a variety of specific forms

VISUAL COMMUNICATION
Represent Ideas Visually
- create a variety of media works

**LINK TO CURRICULUM**

LANGUAGE ARTS
Find Out About a Poet

THE ARTS
Choose Music for a Poem
Make a Pet Poetry Book

MATHEMATICS
Conduct a Survey

## Key Learning Expectations

Students will
- read a variety of fiction and non-fiction materials for different purposes **(Reading Focus, p. 86)**
- state their own interpretation of a written work, using evidence from the work and from their own knowledge and experience **(Reading Mini Lesson, p. 87)**
- produce pieces of writing using a variety of specific forms (poetry) **(Writing Mini Lesson, p. 88)**
- create a variety of media works (illustrations) **(Visual Communication Mini Lesson, p. 88)**

## LINK TO EXPERIENCE

### Read Poems About Pets

Invite students to find poems about pets to share with the class. They can read the poems aloud or add them to the classroom library for others to read.

### Make Pet Word Webs

Have small groups brainstorm words or phrases that describe a pet of their choice. They could organize their ideas in categories and create an illustrated word web about the pet, perhaps using computer graphics software. Encourage students to compare their webs to see commonalities and differences among pets.

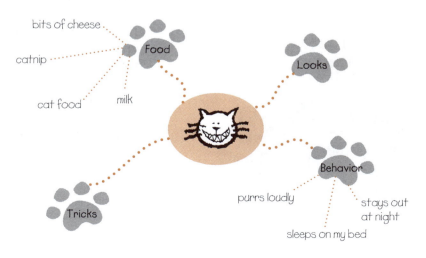

*Pet Poems* 85

## Get Ready to Read

Ask students to scan the poems to determine what pets they will be reading about. Students who have, or used to have, these pets could talk about their experiences. Have students read and listen to the poems to find out more.

# Read and Respond to Text

## Reading Focus

Use a **listen and visualize** strategy. Read "Pony in Moonlight" aloud to the students, inviting them to visualize the scene painted through the words of the poem. Encourage students to share what they pictured. Then, read the poem again. This time, have students listen for phrases that describe what the pony is doing in the moonlight and how it is feeling. Write the lines from the poem on the board and discuss what the phrase "and the owl hoots by" adds to the reading.

Use the same strategy for "My Olympic Tabby Cat." The first time you read the poem to the students, have them picture what the cat is doing. The second time, students can listen to determine why this cat is called an Olympic tabby cat. Discuss the metaphors "bronze medal" and "the gold."

Students can read the other poems with a partner, reading each selection twice. The first time they would listen for a general picture and the second time they would listen for specific information. For example:
- in "Hamsters" students can listen for information about what hamsters look like.
- in "My Fishes" they could listen for the colors of the goldfish.
- in "Rabbit Poem" they could listen for something about rabbits that they especially like.

After reading the poems, partners can talk about the pictures they imagined and about the words that helped them visualize.

## Reader Response

Students could
- hold a conversation about the poems, using questions such as the following as a guide:
  – **Which poem do you prefer? Why?**
  – **Does the poem make you think of a pet that you know?**
  – **How do these poems compare with other poems about pets that you've read?**
  – **If you could choose one of these animals as a pet, which would you choose? Why?**
- draw or paint a picture showing what they visualized while listening to one of the poems.
- have a poetry reading time during which students in small groups read the poems to one another.
- write in their literature response journals about whether they and the poets imagined pets in the same way.

86   Collections 4

# REVISIT THE TEXT

## Reading

### Identify Poetic Techniques

Revisit the poems with the students to build on their knowledge of techniques that poets use for effect. Use specific examples in the poems to elicit, discuss, and chart poetic elements.

### Pet Poems

| | Pony in Moonlight | My Olympic Tabby Cat | Hamsters | My Fishes | Rabbit Poem |
|---|---|---|---|---|---|
| Personification | | cat is compared to an Olympic athlete; dancing leaves; leaves race | | | |
| Simile | | | | goldfish swim like bits of light | |
| Metaphor | moonlight drips | paw is compared to a bat; autumn leaves are compared to bronze and gold medals | | | |
| Alliteration | double dapples | | | | whiskers wiggle |
| Play on words | | | | | to munch on grass is what he's <u>hare</u> for |
| Rhyme | rhyme, but no predictable pattern | no rhyme | last word in second and fourth lines of each stanza rhyme | last word in first and second lines rhyme; last word in third and fourth lines rhyme | some words rhyme, but no predictable pattern |

Students can review the chart to note the variety of poetic techniques used. To apply their learning, they could

- experiment with one of the techniques, using a pet poem as the basis for their writing. For example, they might write similes such as "A pony's neigh is as shrill as _____" or "A hamster's fur is as soft as _____."
- revisit other poems in *Fur, Feathers, Scales, and Skin* to find additional examples of these techniques.
- begin a chart with definitions of the techniques and add other techniques as they discover them in their reading.

*Pet Poems* **87**

## Writing

### Write a Pet Poem

*Learning Strategy Card 38*

Invite students to write a poem, or a stanza of a poem, about one of the pets they read about in the selection. Some students may prefer to write about another animal that interests them, perhaps one from the anthology.

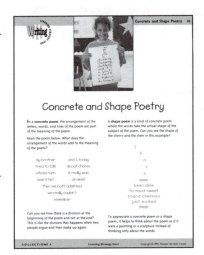

Talk with the students about different forms for their poem. For example, they might imitate the pattern of "Pony in Moonlight," "Hamsters," or the second and third verses of "Rabbit Poem."

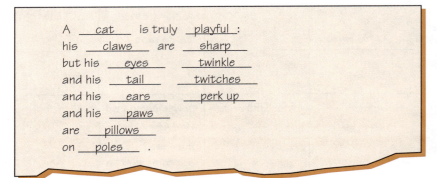

Other students may wish to experiment with more visual forms of poetry such as acrostic poetry. (See *Acrostic Poetry*, Learning Strategy Card 9, for a model.) Or, you might introduce students to concrete poetry and shape poetry, using Learning Strategy Card 38 as a guide.

Encourage students to share their work with one another and to talk about how they wrote the poem and what different techniques they might try next time.

 See **Assess Learning**, page 90.

## Visual Communication

### Represent Ideas Visually

Select a poem in which students seemed to enjoy the rhythm and figurative language. Read the poem again, inviting students to listen for a part that they especially like. Encourage them to picture that part of the poem as words flowing across the page in a pattern. Ask what background colors the words bring to mind.

You might model the visualization process by choosing an image that you particularly like and explaining how you picture the words. For example, for "the leaves dance higher" in "My Olympic Tabby Cat," you might imagine a background of fall colors—reds, oranges, and yellows—with the words written in a flowing musical staff that starts near the bottom of the page and moves higher up.

Encourage students to draw what they visualized. Some students may wish to use water colors to make a color wash on a sheet of paper, then use marking pens to write the part of the poem that they liked over the background. Other students might experiment with computer paint programs instead.

Provide time for students to share and compare their ideas. They could also examine published poetry collections to see how similar ideas are portrayed.

## LINK TO CURRICULUM

### Language Arts

#### Find Out About a Poet

Encourage students to find out about favorite poets. These may be poets whose work students read in this and other collections, family members, or schoolmates whose poems the students enjoy. In small groups, students can read a poem by the poet and share information they gathered.

### The Arts

#### Choose Music for a Poem

Students could work in small groups to prepare a poetry presentation for one of the "Pet Poems" or for a poem of their choice. Encourage them to select a piece of music that will complement the rhythm and mood of the poem. The groups can present their poems to the class or record them on audiotape.

#### Make a Pet Poetry Book

Interested students might decide on five pet poems that they would include in a mini-collection similar to "Pet Poems." Encourage them to illustrate their choices and send them to the language arts department of Prentice Hall Ginn Canada, along with a letter explaining their choices.

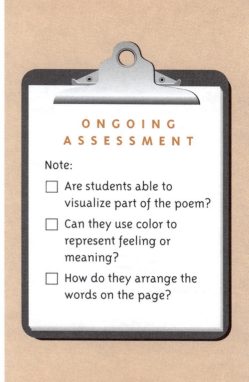

**ONGOING ASSESSMENT**

Note:
- [ ] Are students able to visualize part of the poem?
- [ ] Can they use color to represent feeling or meaning?
- [ ] How do they arrange the words on the page?

Students could write to Prentice Hall Ginn Canada at the following address:
Language Arts Department
Prentice Hall Ginn Canada
1870 Birchmount Road
Scarborough, Ontario
M1P 2J7

### Mathematics

**Conduct a Survey**

Have students conduct a survey to find out what type of pet the class would most like to have. They could base their survey on the pets mentioned in the poems as well as in "You Asked About Pets" (*Fur, Feathers, Scales, and Skin*, p. 68). Encourage students to display the results of their survey in a pictograph.

## Assess Learning

### Writing  (see p. 88)

Assess the pet poems that the students chose to write. Use the **criteria** on *Acrostic Poetry*, Learning Strategy Card 9, and *Concrete and Shape Poetry*, Learning Strategy Card 38, to guide assessment of these forms.

Encourage students to make a **reflective comment** about the task, using prompts similar to those shown.

**Pet Poetry Writing**

1. Topic I chose: _____
   Why I chose it: _____

2. Form I chose: _____
   Why I chose it: _____

3. How I feel about what I wrote: _____

4. What I learned about writing poetry: _____

5. What I'd like to try next time: _____

90   Collections 4

# THEME: PEOPLE AND PETS

Anthology, pages 79–80

> **Special Jobs, Special People** — *a personal narrative*
>
> **Horses** — *a poem*
>
> **Rescue K-9-1** — *a personal narrative*

## LINK TO THE THEME

After reading the selections, students could
- talk with a partner about how each title relates to the theme of pets.
- record in their journals what they like about the selections, for example, the play on words in the title "Rescue K-9-1."

## LINK TO THE WRITING PROCESS

### Write a Newspaper Article

Students could rewrite the story in "Special Jobs, Special People" or "Rescue K-9-1" as a newspaper article about saving a dog. (See *Newspaper Article*, Learning Strategy Card 34, for a model.)

Students might exchange articles with a partner and comment on parts of the writing they liked and parts that could be improved.

### Language Workshop — Usage

- use correctly the conventions of usage (root words, suffixes)

*Blackline Master 20*

#### Teach/Explore/Discover

Write the following sentences on the board or overhead transparency and read them aloud:

- page 79, "Their dog followed on the ice, strutting *lazily* about."
- page 79, "Pooh brought joy and love to our family for 15 1/2 *wonderful* years."
- page 80, " 'No,' I put in *jokingly*, 'Rescue K-9-1'!"

Help students understand that each underlined word is made up of a root word and a suffix. Explain that the suffix gives the word new meaning. Use different-colored chalk or markers to highlight the root and suffix of each word. With "lazily," print the root word "lazy" and the suffix "-ly." Point out that when root words end in "-y," you change the "y" to "i" before adding a suffix.

Together, make a list of other words with the suffixes "-ly" and "-ful," and determine what each suffix means.

> -ful: full of, with the qualities of
> -ly: in a certain way

#### Practise/Apply

Students could
- complete *Suffixes*, Blackline Master 20.
- begin a class chart of words that have suffixes, highlighting the suffix with colored markers.

## LINK TO THE WRITER

After students read what Meredith says about writing, they could conduct a survey to find out whether their classmates prefer to write poetry, short stories, or other literary forms.

*Student Writing* 91

# Using the Genre Books and Novels

## Learning Expectations

Students will
1. Read a variety of fiction and non-fiction materials for different purposes
2. Identify and describe elements of stories
3. Retell a story by adapting it for presentation in another way

## Strategies for Book Connections and Study

### Literature Response Journal

Students can write in their journals following the first reading or keep notes throughout the reading experience.

Suggest that they write
- impressions about the story or the characters.
- questions about parts they didn't understand.
- notes about things that surprised them.

### Reading Workshop

Following the first reading, ask students who read the same book to form small workshop groups. They could begin by
- talking about their favorite parts of the book.
- posing questions about parts they didn't understand or that surprised them.

Guide each group to develop a collaborative plan for focusing their workshops over a few days.

## Approaching the Books

- Arrange the students in four groups, with each group reading a different book.
- Students could preview the books to self-select the one that they would like to read or read the book that best fits their reading level (see pages 6–7).
- Following the book "study," the groups could exchange books and read the other books as part of personal reading if they wish.

### Our Reading Workshop Plan

**Day 1 – Discuss characters**
- Who are they?
- What are they like?
- Who do they remind us of?

**Day 2 – Discuss plot**
- What surprised us in the plot?
- Did the plot turn out the way we thought it would?
- How would we change the plot?

**Day 3 – Share reactions**
- We will take turns sharing and discussing together our journal notes.

**Day 4 – Read aloud our favorite parts**

**PACING TIP**

Use the books as a group book exploration and study during the last two weeks of the unit.

The Reader Response activities in each teaching plan provide other ideas for workshops.

# Gaddy's Story

An Atlantic cod uses first-person narration and photographs of magnifications to tell about its first weeks of life. This non-fiction procedural text relates most closely to the topic focus of animals in the wild (see pages 6–7).

## INTRODUCING THE BOOK

### Share Information About Fish

With students, make a class list of different types of fish. Categorize the fish according to whether they live in salt water or fresh water. Then, invite students to tell what they know about the growth and behavior of fish, eliciting such terms as "minnows," "gills," "fins," and "spawning."

### Recall "Lily Pad Pond"

Ask students to think back on or skim over "Lily Pad Pond" (*Fur, Feathers, Scales, and Skin*, p. 14), noting that it uses text and photographs to show the development of the bullfrog. Review the concept of life cycles and suggest that students keep this in mind when reading *Gaddy's Story* to discover similarities between the two selections.

## CONNECTING WITH THE BOOK

### Explore Book Features

Prior to reading, ask students to look at the book and note features such as the following:
- the cover and title page
- the illustrations and photographs of magnifications
- the song and additional notes
- the acknowledgements
- the information about the author

Invite students to talk about how the author's background might have helped her write the book.

### Reading Focus

Students could use the **read and paraphrase** strategy to talk about the photographs and text, and to share their questions. **(See Activity 1.)**

> Activities on the next two pages serve as guides to focus students' reading and response. The pages can be duplicated and made into transparencies, response sheets, or activity cards.

---

### A SUGGESTED APPROACH TO READING THE BOOKS

Provide time for at least two readings:

#### First Reading

The main goal of the first reading is to provide students with a satisfying reading experience along with a general understanding of the book.

Students who are at the **fluent stage** could read the entire text on their own, pausing to discuss portions of the text as they wish.

Students who would benefit from more **guidance** could use the strategy targeted for the selection.

#### Further Readings

As students engage in further readings, they will deepen and extend their understanding and appreciation through a more detailed exploration of the book.

*Gaddy's Story* 93

**Read *Gaddy's Story***

In this non-fiction text, an Atlantic cod named Gaddy tells you in his own words about his first few weeks of life.

With a partner, take turns reading one or two pages aloud. Each time you change readers, stop and talk about the story. You could

- look at the photographs and discuss what you see.
- make a few notes in your literature response journal, telling what you learned.
- ask each other about anything you didn't understand.

Stop reading after Gaddy's Song. Use what you read and saw in the photographs to draw a diagram of a young Atlantic cod. Label these parts:

| head | tail | eyes | earstones |
| colour cells | fins | muscles | |

Check your diagram with the one on the Additional Notes page. Then, read the notes and record other information you learned.

*Gaddy's Story*   ☐ read a variety of fiction and non-fiction materials for different purposes

# READER RESPONSE

 **Find the Meaning of Fish Words**

Skim *Gaddy's Story* to find words about fish like "earstones," "yolk sac," "colour cells," "spawning," and "zooplankton." Find out what these words mean and why they're important to the cod. Record your information in a chart. You may want to use a dictionary to check some words.

| Word | Meaning | Why it's important to the cod |
| earstones | something in the cod's head, just under its eyes | helps the cod swim straight and stay right way up in the water |

*Gaddy's Story*

### Sing Gaddy's Song

Sing Gaddy's Song with a small group. You could clap out the rhythm as you say the words, find someone to play the notes and sing the song together, or make up your own tune.

Perform your song for the rest of the class. You might want to play instruments or show pictures of Gaddy while you sing.

*Gaddy's Story*

### Write from an Animal's Point of View

In this story, it seems like Gaddy is talking to you about his first few weeks of life. Write about the life cycle of another animal in the same way that Gaddy tells his story. Draw diagrams to show the different stages in the cycle. Add your story to the classroom library for others to enjoy.

*Gaddy's Story*

### Make a Science Game

Skim through *Gaddy's Story* and jot down ten questions about the Atlantic cod's first few weeks of life. Copy your questions on game cards and write the answers on the back. Make up a question-and-answer game to play with these cards. You might design a board game or create a game show like on television.

*Gaddy's Story*

### Design a Photo Album

Make a photo album that shows how you've changed since you were a baby. Gather pictures from family members and write captions that tell where and when each picture was taken. Add your photo album to a display called "How We've Changed."

*Gaddy's Story*

### Compare *Gaddy's Story* and "Lily Pad Pond"

List at least three ways that *Gaddy's Story* and "Lily Pad Pond" (*Fur, Feathers, Scales, and Skin*, p. 14) are the same and three ways that they're different. You might think about these questions:

- What is each selection about?
- Who is the narrator?
- How is the information presented?
- What special features does each selection have?

Compare your work with a partner's and talk about which selection you prefer, and why.

*Gaddy's Story*

# Dragon in the Rocks

In this story based on the childhood of early paleontologist Mary Anning, Marie Day describes a twelve-year-old girl's discovery of important dinosaur fossils in the cliffs around Lyme Regis, England. This biography relates most closely to the topic focus of people's interactions with wild animals (see pages 6–7).

## INTRODUCING THE BOOK

### Write About Future Ambitions

Invite students to think about what they would like to do when they grow up. They could write in their journals about what their job might be, the kinds of things they would do in that job, and why they would choose that occupation. Some students may wish to share their journal entries with one another.

### Recall "Digging Up Dinosaurs"

Ask students to skim "Girl finds dinosaur fossil" in "Digging Up Dinosaurs" (*Fur, Feathers, Scales, and Skin*, p. 57) to recall the discovery of a dinosaur fossil by 12-year-old Tess Owen and her plans to be a paleontologist or zoologist. Encourage students to talk with a partner about what it would be like to be a paleontologist or zoologist, and about the qualities that a paleontologist or zoologist might have.

Suggest that students keep Tess Owen's discovery and future hopes in mind as they read about Mary Anning in *Dragon in the Rocks* to identify similarities between the two young paleontologists.

## CONNECTING WITH THE BOOK

### Explore Book Features

Prior to reading, ask students to look at the book and note features such as the following:
- the cover and title page, including the subtitle
- the copyright page, with Mary Anning's years of birth and death
- the illustrations
- the information about Mary Anning at the end of the book
- the back cover, with a summary of the book, reviews, and recommendations

Invite students to look at the first three illustrations, noting the characters, their clothing, and their activities, to form a general impression of when and where the story took place.

### Reading Focus

Have students use the **double look** strategy to first follow the main storyline and then sequence the important events. **(See Activity 1.)**

> Activities on the next two pages serve as guides to focus students' reading and response. The pages can be duplicated and made into transparencies, response sheets, or activity cards.

96  Collections 4

**Read *Dragon in the Rocks***

This biography tells the story of Mary Anning, a 12-year-old paleontologist who digs out the fossil of an ichthyosaur from a seaside cliff.

Read this book the first time to enjoy the story told through words and pictures. Talk with a partner about important events from the story. Then, skim through the book to check the order of these events. Choose six of the most important events to draw in a story wheel.

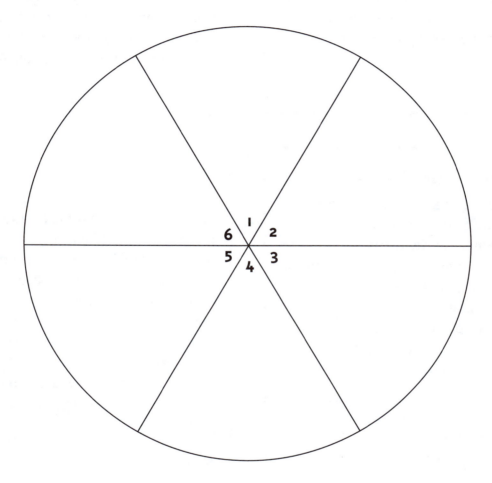

Make a cover for your story circle.
- Trace a circle the same size as the first.
- Cut out one pie-sized shape.
- Place your new circle over the story circle.
- Use a pencil to make a small hole in the middle of the two circles.
- Attach the two circles with a fastener.
- Write the title of the story and the author's name on the cover.

Turn the open space to the first story event. Invite a classmate to retell *Dragon in the Rocks* using your story circle.

*Dragon in the Rocks* ☐ retell a story by adapting it for presentation in another way (create wheel)

## Write About Mary Anning

In the story, you learned about Mary Anning by what she said and did. Look at the copyright page to find out when she was born and when she died, and read the last page of the book for more information. Jot down at least five things that you learned about Mary, then write a descriptive paragraph or poem about her for others to read.

*Dragon in the Rocks*

 ## Act Out the Story

Together with classmates who have read *Dragon in the Rocks*, choose a part of the story to act out. Plan who will be the narrator and each of the characters, and how you will perform your drama. As you practise your parts, give one another suggestions about how to use your voice and actions to tell the story. When you're ready, act out the story for the rest of the class.

*Dragon in the Rocks*

 ## Make a Jigsaw Puzzle

Draw a picture of a dinosaur scene on a piece of cardboard. On the back, use thick black lines to divide the picture into jigsaw puzzle pieces. Cut apart the puzzle and place the pieces in an envelope. Exchange puzzles with a partner. Put together your partner's puzzle and write a story about the scene you find.

*Dragon in the Rocks*

 ## Find Similes

Mr. Anning says that the creature in the rocks has "teeth like razors" and "eyes as big as saucers." When you use the words "like" or "as" to compare two things, it's called a simile. Record other similes from the story in your literature response journal or write similes to describe other creatures that lived millions of years ago. You might like to draw a picture to go with your simile. Share your work with a partner.

*Dragon in the Rocks*

 ## Design a Character Hat

Reread the part of the story that tells about Captain Fossy's plumed hat. Design a hat for another character in the book. Use different materials from the classroom such as paper plates, crêpe paper, construction paper, and scraps of cloth. Your hat could show something about the character's personality or activities, or you might decorate it with items that are important to the character.

*Dragon in the Rocks*

 ## Visit a Museum

Visit a local museum. Jot down notes and questions about a display that catches your interest. Ask someone who works at the museum for more information, or find out more from books, magazines, videos, or computer software.

*Dragon in the Rocks*

# Lost and Found

Lucy makes her first friend in a new town—a stray dog named Trouble. But when her parents and the girl down the street begin to look for Trouble's owner, Lucy realizes that she may lose her new friend. This novel relates most closely to the topic focus of people and pets (see pages 6–7).

## INTRODUCING THE BOOK

### Brainstorm Ways to Advertise

Invite students to brainstorm different ways to advertise a lost pet. Elicit suggestions such as displaying posters in supermarkets, in libraries, or on utility poles, or submitting an announcement to a local radio station's lost and found segment. Record students' ideas on a chart and encourage them to add to the list as they read the novel.

### Recall "Keeping Old Friends"

Ask students to think back on, or skim, "Keeping Old Friends" (*Fur, Feathers, Scales, and Skin*, p. 72) to recall how much Holly meant to the family and how they felt when she died. Together, make a list of words that describe the family's feelings and actions. Students can keep the list in mind as they look at the cover of *Lost and Found* and suggest what the story might be about and what different emotions might be involved.

## CONNECTING WITH THE BOOK

### Explore Book Features

Prior to reading, ask students to look over the book and note features such as the following:
- the story summary on the inside page and back cover
- the title and copyright page
- the dedication and acknowledgements
- the table of contents, noting that there are 17 numbered and named chapters
- the summary of *Mama's Going to Buy You a Mockingbird*, also by Jean Little

Invite students to read the story summary on the back cover, as well as the Contents page, to confirm or revise the predictions they made based on the front cover.

### Reading Focus

Students can use a **follow along** strategy as they read this book independently or with a partner, thinking about the important events of the story and the characters' feelings. **(See Activity 1.)**

> Activities on the next two pages serve as guides to focus students' reading and response. The pages can be duplicated and made into transparencies, response sheets, or activity cards.

**Read *Lost and Found***

In this novel, Mary moves to a new town and makes her first friend—a stray dog named Trouble. But when her parents start wondering whether Trouble is really a stray, Mary realizes that she may not be able to keep the dog as her own.

Read the story on your own or with a partner, using the Follow Along Grid below as a guide. Write or draw your responses in your literature response journal or talk about them with your partner.

| READ THESE CHAPTERS | THINK ABOUT OR DRAW THESE THINGS |
|---|---|
| Read chapters 1, 2, 3, and 4 to find out about the dog on the front cover. | 1. Why do you think the little dog was so important to Lucy?<br><br>2. Tell about a time when you felt lonely and sad like Lucy. |
| Read chapters 5, 6, 7, and 8 to find out how the girl at the end of chapter 4 is involved with the story. | 3. Why do you think that Nan didn't notice how Lucy felt about the dog?<br><br>4. List the things that people have done so far to find Trouble's owner. How do you think this made Lucy feel? |
| Read chapters 9, 10, 11, and 12 to find out about further progress in finding Trouble's owner. | 5. Make two lists: one of the happy moments and the other of the sad moments Lucy had in these chapters.<br><br>6. How do you think Lucy felt when her father told her about the telephone call from the animal shelter? |
| Read chapters 13, 14, 15, 16, and 17 to find out what happened with Lucy. | 7. Put yourself in Andy's place. Jot down some of the things you'd be thinking as you held Trouble in your arms.<br><br>8. Draw a picture of the event in these chapters that you liked the best. |

What is the turning point in the story? Why do you think that?

*Lost and Found*

☐ identify and describe elements of stories (charcters, plot)

100    COLLECTIONS 4 Copyright © 1999 Prentice Hall Ginn Canada. Permission to reproduce this page is restricted to the purchasing school.

# READER RESPONSE

 **Make a Poster**

Make a Dog Found poster to help you find Trouble's owner. Draw a picture of Trouble and write what he looks like and how he acts. Include information about who the owners should contact if they think this is their dog.

*Lost and Found*

 **Do a Dramatic Reading**

With some classmates, choose a favorite chapter to read aloud to another group. Each person decides which part to read. Use your voices to show how the characters are feeling and to help listeners feel like they're part of the story. Ask your audience which part of the chapter they liked best, and why.

*Lost and Found*

 **Write About Lucy and Nan's Friendship**

Skim through the story to find parts that tell about Lucy and Nan's friendship. Make a list of the things they did together and think about how Lucy felt about Nan. Then, talk with a partner about whether you think that Lucy and Nan will stay friends.

*Lost and Found*

 **Read the Acknowledgements Page**

Reread the acknowledgements page to find out about Jean Little's struggles as a writer and about the support that people gave her. Then, write in your literature response journal about a time when you found it difficult to write and how people helped or encouraged you.

*Lost and Found*

 **Read Other Books by Jean Little**

Choose another book to read on your own.
*Hey World, Here I Am!* Kids Can Press, 1986.
*Different Dragons.* Penguin Books, 1986.
*From Anna.* Harper Trophy, 1973.
*Mama's Going to Buy You a Mockingbird.* Puffin, 1986.

*Lost and Found*

 **Tell About Your Choice of Dogs**

Use the descriptions of the dogs in chapters 15 and 16 to help you decide which dog you would choose, and why. Draw what you think the dog looks like. Show your picture to a partner and compare your choices and reasons.

*Lost and Found*

# Pelly

A young girl forms a unique bond with a pelican in this touching story about overcoming loneliness and making new friends. This novel relates most closely to the topic focus of people's interactions with wild animals (see pages 6–7).

## INTRODUCING THE BOOK

### Record Information About Pelicans

Invite students to record questions that they have about pelicans. Small groups might use various print and non-print resources to research some of these questions and record the answers in a fact chart. Students could refer to this information as they read *Pelly* and confirm or add to what they learned.

### Recall "Interview with Father Goose"

Ask students to recall, or skim, "Interview with Father Goose" (*Fur, Feathers, Scales, and Skin*, p. 62) to think about why it's important for birds to migrate south in the winter and what difficulties they will experience if they stay in cold northern climates. Students might also recall the relationship between Bill Lishman and the geese. Suggest that students keep these thoughts in mind while they read *Pelly* to discover connections between the two selections.

## CONNECTING WITH THE BOOK

### Explore Book Features

Prior to reading, ask students to look over the novel and note features such as the following:
- the cover and title page
- the copyright page and dedication
- the division into chapters that are numbered but not named
- the book summary
- information about the author and illustrator

Invite students to read the book summary and talk with a partner about whether or not Sandra will be able to keep the pelican alive during the bitterly cold Prairie winter. Students might draw or write about something they think might happen to Pelly.

### Reading Focus

Students could use a **read and reflect** strategy, stopping at the end of each chapter to reflect on the setting of the story, the story events, and the characters. **(See Activity 1.)**

> Activities on the next two pages serve as guides to focus students' reading and response. The pages can be duplicated and made into transparencies, response sheets, or activity cards.

**Read *Pelly***

In this novel, a young girl becomes friends with a pelican that stays behind while the rest of the flock migrates south for the winter.

Read the first chapter aloud with other students who are reading *Pelly*. In a chart, describe the setting, character, and important events. Write a title for the chapter that tells the main idea but that doesn't give everything away.

> Chapter: 1   Title: At the Waterfall
>
> Setting: by the riverbank
>
> Characters: Sandra, three kids (two boys and a girl), pelicans
>
> Important events:
> - a redheaded boy wants to catch pelicans and have them stuffed—he'd get $25 for each pelican
> - Sandra watches the pelicans—one comes right up to her

Take turns reading Chapters 2—25 with a partner. You might read the book in these sections.

| | | |
|---|---|---|
| Chapters 2 and 3 | Chapters 4, 5, 6, and 7 | Chapters 8, 9, 10, and 11 |
| Chapters 12, 13, 14, and 15 | Chapters 16, 17, 18, and 19 | Chapters 20, 21, and 22 |
| Chapters 23, 24, and 25 | | |

For each chapter, fill out a chart like the one above.

Before reading the last chapter, predict how the story might end. Then, meet with the whole group to read Chapter 26 and talk about whether the story turned out as you expected.

*Pelly*                                                                                          ☐ identify and describe elements of stories

# READER RESPONSE

 **Illustrate a Chapter**

Sometimes, the chapters in a novel start with an illustration. The illustration usually shows something that is going to happen, without giving away important events.

Choose a chapter in *Pelly* that you would like to illustrate. First, draw some sketches of what you might want to show. Then, choose one sketch that you think would suit the beginning of the chapter. Draw your illustration in the same style as the drawings in the story.

*Pelly*

## 3  Chart Pelly's Problems

With a partner, think of all the problems that Pelly had. You might want to skim parts of the story to check. Chapters 1, 3, 11, and 26 describe one problem that keeps appearing, while Chapters 6, 8, 18, 19, 22, 23, and 24 describe other problems. Jot down the problems, numbering them in the order that they happened, and write how they turned out.

Make a problem map for the story by drawing one circle for each problem. Write about the problem and its solution inside the circle, then join the circles with short lines. Be sure the problems are in the order that they happened.

Use your problem map to tell a classmate about the story.

*Pelly*

 ## 6  Read Other Animal Adventure Stories

Choose another animal adventure story to read on your own.

*Jacob's Little Giant*. Barbara Smucker. Penguin, 1987.
*The Wilds of Whip-Poor-Will Farm*. Janet Foster. Firefly Books, 1992.
*The Midnight Fox*. Betsy Byars. Penguin, 1981.
*The Mare on the Hill*. Thomas Locker. Puffin, 1995.
*Charlotte's Web*. E. B. White. HarperCollins Children's Books, 1952.

*Pelly*

 ## 4  Write a Tall Tale

Ernie tells five different tall tales about the missing part of his finger. Make up your own tall tale to explain what might have happened. Check Chapters 7, 9, 10, 15, and 25 to review the stories Ernie told. Make sure your story is different. Present your story in an Author's Chair. (See *Author's Chair*, Learning Strategy Card 17, for a model.)

*Pelly*

 ## 5  Compare Migrating Birds

Brainstorm different birds that migrate. Choose one and compare it with the pelican. Find out what the pelican and the bird you chose look like, where they live, what they eat, and how they behave. Make a chart to show the similarities and differences.

*Pelly*

 ## 7  Read Chapter Endings

The last paragraph of a chapter is supposed to make readers want to read on. Reread the last paragraph of a few chapters in *Pelly*. Jot down chapter endings that keep your interest and explain why they work well. You might use some of these ideas as you write your own book.

*Pelly*

# Concluding Connections and Study for the Genre Books and Novels

## 1. Share Small Group Learnings

Provide time for each book connections and study group to
- share their book, through a book talk or dramatization.
- lead a discussion on the ideas and topics in the book.
- tell how their book connects to the *Fur, Feathers, Scales, and Skin* anthology selections and to the ideas encountered in the unit.
- do an oral reading of a section of the book.
- share some of their Reader Response activities.

## 2. Hold a Whole Class Conversation

Help students synthesize and summarize the understandings they have about their books by choosing questions similar to the following ones. Encourage response to each question from all members of all of the book connection and study groups.

### Questions for discussion

- Do you like the title the author chose for the book? Why? Why not? Does it give you an idea of what animal is involved in the story?
- Who is the main character(s)? How is the animal involved in the story?
- Are the characters like any of the characters that you met in *Fur, Feathers, Scales, and Skin*? Which ones? How are they the same? How are they different?
- Does the story remind you of any experiences you've had with animals? Tell what happened.
- What connections are there between this book and the books that your classmates read?

You might choose one question a day for a period of five days to either begin or end the class. Post the question a day ahead of time so that students can prepare their ideas and draw upon specific references in their respective books.

## 3. Make a Personal Response

Provide prompts such as the following for students to write. They could
- choose a part of the story to rewrite from another point of view.
- write a different story ending, making sure it fits with earlier information and events.
- write information for a pamphlet or flyer to advertise the book.
- write a personal opinion about the book, telling
  - how they felt about the book.
  - who would like the book.
  - about a part that stands out in their minds.
  - what they would change, add, or take away.

Students' writing could be assessed and placed in their portfolios as one record of their understanding of the book.

*Genre Books and Novels*  105

# Assess the Unit

Throughout the unit, there are many opportunities for ongoing assessment and celebration of what students have learned and accomplished in guided mini-lessons and in individual or small group activities.

## Ongoing Observations

Consolidate ongoing observations that you have noted for each student using the "Ongoing Assessment" boxes, your observation of literature discussions, group discussions, .... Use the *Observation Record Master* (*Assessment Handbook*) to help you consolidate your comments.

## Unit Assessment Checklist

Use the *Assess Working Style and Attitudes Assessment Master* (*Assessment Handbook*) to help you assess performance on attitudes. Use *Appendix 1* (pp. 138–139) in this book to help you assess and record student performance.

## Gather and Record Assessment Information and Data

**ASSESSMENT SUGGESTIONS**

The *COLLECTIONS 4 Assessment Handbook* contains many suggestions and reproducible forms to assist with assessment and evaluation.

### 1. Reading

Use the **Fur, Feathers, Scales, and Skin** *Reading Passages Assessment Masters* (*Assessment Handbook*). Students can read and respond to either the prose passage or the poem or to both passages. The *Handbook* describes how to choose the passages, how to conduct the activity, and criteria for scoring.

### 2. Writing

Students could submit one piece of writing of their choice for assessment.

Procedures and criteria for assessing the writing can be found in the *Assessment Handbook*.

### 3. Sample of Students' Learning for Portfolios

Review and assess learning records such as the following:
- logs of books students have read (*Reading Log Assessment Master, Assessment Handbook*)
- spelling and vocabulary pretests and post tests

- writing portfolios, including pieces of writing started or completed
- displays, models, scientific diagrams, and artwork
- research reports
- webs, charts, notes crafted by students
- tapes of oral reading, oral presentations, or reports
- assignments of work or worksheets demonstrating performance on specific literacy tasks (such as those identified in "Assess Learning" activities noted throughout the unit)

Choose samples that will remain in the assessment portfolio as a record of student performance on the unit.

### 4. Self-Assessment

Students could
- **write in their learning logs** what they have learned about the world of animals and people's interactions with them.
- **write a self-assessment report or "can do" list** to describe what they have learned. They might benefit from using the *Thinking Back on the Unit Assessment Master* (*Assessment Handbook*) containing prompts or lead-in phrases to help them focus on aspects of their learning.

They can use what they have prepared to help them plan what skills they need to work on in the next unit.

### 5. Teacher-Student Conferences

Throughout the unit, take opportunities to talk with individual students to see how they are progressing in personal reading and writing. Use or adapt
- *Questions to Guide a Personal Reading Conference Assessment Master* (*Assessment Handbook*) to help you conduct a **reading conference.**
- *Questions to Guide a Personal Writing Conference Assessment Master* (*Assessment Handbook*) to help you conduct a **writing conference.**

---

**AT THE END OF AN ACTIVITY OR UNIT**

*My Self-Assessment Report*

The book I found the most interesting was <u>Dragon in the Rocks</u> because I like looking for fossils. I even have my own fossil collection! The first fossil I ever found was of a snail. I have fossils of plants, too. My family went to the Burgess Shale in Yoho National Park in Alberta and we saw fossils of creatures that lived millions of years ago.

Something that really made me sad was the story "Keeping Old Friends." I know how the family felt when Holly died because we had a dog that died too.

My favorite activity was using computer software to experiment with typography. I tried different fonts and they made my work look more interesting.

I also liked researching how people solve crimes against animals. I might want to work in a wildlife forensics laboratory one day because I like science and animals and I also want to be a detective.

I need to get help writing a book cover synopsis. I always write too much and give the whole story away.

Something else I want to know more about is what happened with Father Goose and the sandhill cranes. I wonder if he got them to migrate from Saskatchewan to South Carolina. I also want to know if he started working with whooping cranes. My brother and I are going to sell lemonade to help raise money for Operation Migration.

# Blackline Masters

Home Connections Newsletter . . . . . . . . . . . . . . . . . . . . . . . . . . . 1 & 2
"The Hare and the Tortoise" . . . . . . . . . . . . . . . . . . . . . . . . . . . . . 3
Who Is Speaking? . . . . . . . . . . . . . . . . . . . . . . . . . . . . . . . . . . . . 4
Change the Order . . . . . . . . . . . . . . . . . . . . . . . . . . . . . . . . . . . . 5
Read, Pause, and Reflect Grid for "The Wounded Wolf" . . . . . . . . . . . 6
Book Summary for "The Wounded Wolf" . . . . . . . . . . . . . . . . . . . . 7
Giving Examples and Reasons . . . . . . . . . . . . . . . . . . . . . . . . . . . . 8
Guided Reading Grid for "From a Whale-Watcher's Diary" . . . . . . . . . 9
Word Pictures . . . . . . . . . . . . . . . . . . . . . . . . . . . . . . . . . . . . . . 10
"Killer Whales Make Cellular Calls!" . . . . . . . . . . . . . . . . . . . 11 & 12
"Musk Oxen" . . . . . . . . . . . . . . . . . . . . . . . . . . . . . . . . . . . . . . 13
Words That Show Time . . . . . . . . . . . . . . . . . . . . . . . . . . . . . . . 14
Verbs in the Past . . . . . . . . . . . . . . . . . . . . . . . . . . . . . . . . . . . 15
Make a 3-D Pet Card . . . . . . . . . . . . . . . . . . . . . . . . . . . . . . . . 16
Read and Reflect Grid for "Keeping Old Friends" . . . . . . . . . . . . . . 17
"The Accident" . . . . . . . . . . . . . . . . . . . . . . . . . . . . . . . . . . . . . 18
Contractions . . . . . . . . . . . . . . . . . . . . . . . . . . . . . . . . . . . . . . 19
Suffixes . . . . . . . . . . . . . . . . . . . . . . . . . . . . . . . . . . . . . . . . . . 20

## Spelling Words Masters

Animal Profiles / Lily Pad Pond . . . . . . . . . . . . . . . . . . . . . . . . . . 21
The Wounded Wolf / From a Whale-Watcher's Diary . . . . . . . . . . . . 22
Animal Crimes, Animal Clues / The Northern Way . . . . . . . . . . . . . 23
The Puff Adder Who Was Stuck / Digging Up Dinosaurs . . . . . . . . . . 24
An Interview with Father Goose / You Asked About Pets . . . . . . . . . . 25
Keeping Old Friends . . . . . . . . . . . . . . . . . . . . . . . . . . . . . . . . . 26

# Fur, Feathers, Scales, and Skin

## Home Connections Newsletter

### About the Unit

Our new unit in language arts is *Fur, Feathers, Scales, and Skin*. For the next month or so, we'll be talking, reading, and writing about the world of animals and people's interactions with them. As we work together, the children will have many opportunities to reflect on their experiences and relationships with the animals around them.

You can help your child make the connection at home. Together, look through this newsletter and choose books to share and activities and homework projects to do.

### Learning Goals

In this unit, your child will

- listen to, read, and talk about selections related to animals and people's interactions with them.
- examine the features of different types of non-fiction text.
- learn to gather and organize information.
- report and document factual information in different ways.
- learn to spell words from personal and class lists.

## BOOK BAG

These stories are about animals and our interactions with them. Look for one or more of these books at your local library for your child to read or to share together.

*Beautiful Joe* by Marshall Saunders. This novel, based on a real dog, tells how Beautiful Joe finally finds a happy home after being mistreated.

*Fantastic Mr. Fox* by Roald Dahl. Three rascally farmers nearly wreck the countryside trying to get rid of wily Mr. Fox and his family.

*The Fur Person* by May Sarton. Tom Jones, an independent cat-about-town, moves in with two elderly ladies and learns to be a loving pet, known as a "fur person."

*The Incredible Journey* by Sheila Burnford. Luath the Labrador, Tao the Siamese cat, and Bodger the bull terrier make their way across the wilderness to find their owners.

*Pit Pony* by Joyce Barkhouse. Life in a coal mine becomes more tolerable for eleven-year-old Willie when he starts working with a pony he loves.

### Plan a Family Outing

With your child and other family members, plan a visit to a place where you can learn about animals, for example, a pond, a zoo, or a veterinarian's office. Draw a picture of what you saw, build a model, or make an audiotape.

Your child has been reading stories, articles, and poems about animals and people's interactions with them. Together, talk about a selection that your child liked and ask him/her to draw or tell about a favorite part.

*COLLECTIONS 4* Copyright © 1999 Prentice Hall Ginn Canada.
Permission to reproduce this page is restricted to the purchasing school.

HOME CONNECTIONS NEWSLETTER

# Fur, Feathers, Scales, and Skin
## Home Connections Newsletter

# Homemade Fun

## Talk Time

At mealtime, talk about some of the following questions that arise from the reading selections in the unit.

- If you could have any kind of pet you wanted, what would you choose? Why? How would other family members react?
- What endangered animals do you know about? What do you think should be done to protect them?
- What animal would you like to see in its natural habitat? What interests you about that animal?
- Do you know any amazing stories about animals and people getting along together, or about two unlikely animals becoming friends? Share your stories.

## Follow the News

With your family, gather news about animals from sources such as television and radio broadcasts, newspaper and magazine articles, and the Internet. You might wish to post the news on a special bulletin board or on the refrigerator, or you could talk about it during a family talk time.

## Play a Game

Make an outdoor beanbag toss or hopscotch game by having your child write his/her spelling words in squares on a concrete drive or walkway with multicolored chalk.

## Homework Projects

**Week 1 — Create an "Animal Facts" mini-booklet.**
Make a mini-booklet with an interesting fact about 10 different animals. Include a drawing, sticker, or magazine picture of the animal on each page.

**Week 2 — Observe animals around you.**
With a family member, take an observation walk each day around an area near your home. List the animals you see and make short notes about them. At the end of the week, organize your notes into an observation record.

**Week 3 — Answer the question: Is there a problem with animals in your neighborhood?**
Ask at least five people for their opinions. Tape-record or jot down their suggestions for ways to solve the problem that would be fair to the animals. Play your tape in class or discuss the responses.

**Week 4 — Make a 3-D animal.**
Use natural or recycled materials, such as pine cones, twigs, or small boxes, to create an animal. Display the model in the classroom.

*COLLECTIONS 4* Copyright © 1999 Prentice Hall Ginn Canada.
Permission to reproduce this page is restricted to the purchasing school.

# The Hare and the Tortoise

A Hare taunted a Tortoise because of the slowness of her pace and boasted of his own great speed. "Then let us have a race," said the Tortoise. "I'll run with you eight kilometres, and the Fox yonder shall be the judge." The Hare agreed and away they went. But in his eagerness to win he started off as fast as he could and soon left the Tortoise far behind. The Hare, tired from his exertions, stopped by the way to take a nap, confident that if the Tortoise went by he could easily overtake her. Meanwhile the resolute Tortoise kept up a slow but steady pace and plodded along. The Hare overslept and awakened to find, when he arrived at the goal, that the Tortoise had reached it just before him.

*Perserverance and determination compensate for the absence of natural gifts.*

Talk about the following questions with your classmates.

1. What lesson does the fable teach? Explain it in your own words.
2. What do you learn about this tortoise?
3. Tell two other things you know about tortoises.

# WHO Is Speaking?

## Cat

The black cat yawns,
Opens her jaws,
Stretches her legs,
And shows her claws.

Then she gets up
And stands on four
Long stiff legs
And yawns some more.

She shows her sharp teeth.
She stretches her lip,
Her slice of a tongue
Turns up at the tip.

Lifting herself
On her delicate toes,
She arches her back
As high as it goes.

She lets herself down
With particular care,
And pads away
With her tail in the air.

— MARY BRITTON MILLER

[from *An Arkful of Animals*, selected
by William Cole. Copyright © 1978,
Houghton Mifflin.]

## Black Beauty (excerpt)

Whilst I was young I lived upon my
mother's milk, as I could not eat grass. In
the day time I ran by her side, and at night I
lay down close by her. When it was hot, we
used to stand by the pond in the shade of
the trees, and when it was cold, we had a
nice warm shed near the plantation.

As soon as I was old enough to eat grass,
my mother used to go out to work in the
day time, and came back in the evening.

There were six young colts in the
meadow beside me. They were older than I
was—some were nearly as large as grownup
horses. I used to run with them, and had
great fun. We used to gallop all together
round the field, as hard as we could go.
Sometimes we had rather rough play, for
they would frequently bite and kick as well
as gallop.

— ANNA SEWELL

Talk about the following questions with a partner:

1 Who is speaking in "Cat"? How do you know?

2 Who is speaking in "Black Beauty"? How do you know?

3 Choose something that you've written in which the main
character could tell the story. Rewrite your story or poem
the way this character would tell it.

*COLLECTIONS 4* Copyright © 1999 Prentice Hall Ginn Canada.
Permission to reproduce this page is restricted to the purchasing school.

DESERT TORTOISE **4**

# Change the Order

Change the word order and write the new sentence.

1. A water strider skates across the surface of the pond.
   _____

2. By morning the dragonfly's wings will be dry enough for it to fly away.
   _____

Arrange the words and phrases into interesting sentences. Begin your sentence with a capital letter. Compare your work with a classmate's.

3. | a painted turtle | across the damp grass |
   | crawled slowly | at dawn |

4. | hopped quickly | the silly bunny |
   | over the sleeping fox | in the grassy field |

5. | black bears | drink nothing |
   | eat nothing and | over the winter |

6. Choose a piece of your writing. Change the word order in some of the sentences.

# Read, Pause, and Reflect Grid
## The Wounded Wolf

Use this grid to guide you as you read the story. At each stopping point, talk about the questions with your group.

| | |
|---|---|
| Read pages 18–19. | **1** How do you think Roko felt as he watched his pack fight the caribou?<br><br>**2** What might happen to Roko with the raven flying overhead? |
| Read pages 20–21. | **3** What might Roko have been thinking as the animals circled around him?<br><br>**4** What extra danger is there now that the grizzly bear is on the scene? |
| Read pages 22–23. | **5** How did you feel after Roko fell? How did you feel when he started to fight back against the other animals?<br><br>**6** What are Roko's chances of survival? What might happen to make a difference? |
| Read pages 24–27. | **7** How do you think Roko felt when Kiglo arrived?<br><br>**8** Did the story end like you thought it would? |

*COLLECTIONS 4* Copyright © 1999 Prentice Hall Ginn Canada.
Permission to reproduce this page is restricted to the purchasing school.

## Book Summary for

# The Wounded Wolf

A gravely wounded wolf limps along Toklat Ridge. "Kong, kong, kong," bells the raven—death is coming to the Ridge. The fox, the snowy owl, the grizzly bear, all join the death watch.

But the wounded wolf is not alone in the Arctic Valley.

Through poetic text, the author tells a story of the closely bound members of the wolf pack and their fellow valley dwellers. John Schoenherr's illustrations perfectly convey the Alaskan scene.

[Book jacket copy from *The Wounded Wolf*, copyright © 1978 by Jean Craighead George. Reprinted with permission.]

Choose a book from the animal book display.

Write your own summary for it.

Make changes to your summary and write the finished version on a card.

Decorate your card as a bookmark.

> A good summary
> - is short.
> - is interesting.
> - doesn't give away all the details.

# Giving Examples and Reasons

In each sentence, underline the **example** that Joseph gives for why wetlands are important and circle the word that introduces the **reason** why people should preserve them.

1. Wetlands should be conserved because they are home to geese, ducks, moose and many other animals.

2. If people stop destroying the wetlands it will increase the amount of drinking water.

Use the words **because** and **if** to complete the sentences.

3. Toads and frogs are helpful _____ they control the number of flies and mosquitoes.

4. The baby birds will go hungry _____ the mother bird doesn't find food.

5. The animals were homeless _____ a fire destroyed the forest.

6. More floods will occur _____ wetlands are destroyed.

7. _____ you destroy the wetlands, many animals will be on the verge of extinction.

8. Choose an animal. Write a paragraph about why it is important to protect this animal. Use words such as **because** and **if** to support your arguments.

# Guided Reading Grid
## From a Whale-Watcher's Diary

Use this grid to guide you as you read the story.

At each stopping point, talk about the questions with your group.

| | |
|---|---|
| Read the information box on the 24-hour clock and the diary entries from 0600 to the end of 0955. | 1 How do you convert from the standard clock to the regular clock?<br><br>2 How does a hydrophone help locate whales? |
| Read the diary entries from 1030 to the end of 1530 and the information box on how whales get their names. | 3 What is surprising about the behavior of A1 pod?<br><br>4 In what two ways do scientists name whales? |
| Read the diary entries from 1545 to the end of 2000 and the information box on echolocation. | 5 What happens when the two whale pods meet in the inlet?<br><br>6 What is echolocation and why is it important to whales? |

As you read, jot down new words that you find.
Add these words to your personal dictionary.

*COLLECTIONS 4* Copyright © 1999 Prentice Hall Ginn Canada.
Permission to reproduce this page is restricted to the purchasing school.

# Word Pictures

In each sentence, circle the words that form pictures in your mind. Choose one sentence and draw the picture.

1. At this time of year the melting glaciers turn the inlet waters pale green and against it the whales look blacker than ever.

2. With just the tips of their dorsal fins showing they look like sharks as they zig-zag up the inlet.

3. He is moving in a circle, lunging out of the water, waving his pectoral fin, fluke slapping, spyhopping, and making sputtering noises on the surface.

4. The sky is streaked deep red and orange with a light west wind blowing.

Add words to these sentences to make vivid pictures.

5. The _____ _____ trees _____ _____ in the _____ .

6. The _____ porpoise _____ and _____ in the _____ _____ water.

7. In the glowing sunset, _____ _____ .

8. Revise a piece of your writing to help the reader see the picture you are describing.

# KILLER WHALES *make cellular calls!*

**At the Aquarium, the phone calls will be piped in "live" to a special area where scientists and students can identify each group of whales by voice-print, and chart their progress along the coast.**

The killer whales who migrate up and down BC's coast don't know it, but they are about to start making cellular phone calls that may one day save their lives.

It's part of a project called *WhaleLink*, first dreamed up 10 years ago by marine biologist Dr. John Ford, of the Vancouver Aquarium. At that time the technology wasn't quite ready. Now, thanks to technical advances, and with help from computer science students from B.C.I.T. (the British Columbia Institute of Technology) and the BC TEL Mobility cellular network, his dream is about to become real.

"Pods of killer whales migrate through Haro and Johnstone Straits heading north to spend the winter," says Dr. Ford. "But we don't really know exactly where they go, so we don't know whether or not we need to be protecting their habitat." ▶

## ENTER THE CELLULAR PHONE CONNECTION.

Dr. Ford's idea is to have underwater microphones (hydrophones) listening for the whale pods. When they pass, the hydrophones will activate cellular phones above the waterline. The cellular phones will automatically call the Aquarium.

At the Aquarium, the phones will be piped in "live" to a special area where scientists, students, and the public can identify each group of whales by their voice-prints, and chart their progress along the coast.

"Each pod has a distinctive sound," says Dr. Ford, "so we know immediately which pod is passing the hydrophone."

Initial trials of San Juan Island and Robson Bight are helping to work out the last few bugs in the system. With enough cellular installations placed along the coast, scientists should be able to track the whales accurately and learn much more about where their winter living areas are.

"The hydrophones have to be able to distinguish whale sounds from all the other sounds underwater," says Dr. Ford. "Right now, passing boats will sometimes activate them if they come too close. We just need to do a bit of fine tuning of the software to eliminate that problem."

Dr. Ford expects *WhaleLink* to be up and swimming within the next six months.

[From *In Touch*. Published by BC TEL Mobility Cellular, Fall 1995.]

Talk with a partner about the information in this article. Use these questions as a guide.

1. Why do you think scientists need to learn more about where whales live in winter?
2. Tell about Dr. Ford's idea in your own words.
3. How else do you think scientists might use cellular phones to help whales and other animals?

You and your partner can share and compare your ideas with another pair.

# Musk Oxen

Yai-yai-yai
Yai-yai-yai
I ran with all speed
And met them on the plain,
The great musk ox with brilliant black hair —
Hayai-ya-haya.

It was the first time I had seen them,
Grazing on the flowers of the plain,
Far from the hill where I stood,
And ignorantly I thought
They were but small and slight …

But they grew up out of the earth
As I came within shot,
Great black giant beasts
Far from our dwellings
In the regions of happy summer hunting.

**– Igjugarjuk**

[from *Songs Are Thoughts: Poems of the Inuit*, selected by Neil Philip. Copyright © 1995, Doubleday Canada Limited.]

Write about the poem in your literature response journal.

1. What is the poet describing?

2. What does this tell you about the northern way of life?

3. Jot down some words and phrases that make the poem come alive.

# Words That Show Time

Here are some words and phrases from "Naomi's Geese" that tell about time.

| at the end | until | finally |
|---|---|---|
| soon | at first | gradually |

Use these words and phrases to complete the following sentences. There may be more than one word that makes sense.

1. _____ Naomi doesn't like the summer house or the two geese that are there.

2. _____ the geese get used to Naomi and stop hissing and running at her.

3. _____ of the summer it was time for the geese to migrate and the people to return to the city.

4. Naomi's loons did not leave _____ there was ice on the pond.

5. Write three sentences using some of the words and phrases below. Read your sentences to a partner.

| tomorrow | when | in the beginning |
|---|---|---|
| later | yesterday | once upon a time |
| before | in a minute | after |

6. Look at a piece of your own writing to find words that tell about time. Add these words to the wall chart your class started or to your personal dictionary.

# Verbs in the Past

 Read the sentences below from "Piping Plover." Underline the verbs that let you know this story happened in the past.

> The rock I saw looked like a bird and I bent down to pick it up. When I looked at it closer, I discovered that it was a bird!!! I expected it to fly away; instead it jumped on the ground and flapped its wing. Right then I knew one of its wings was broken. I brought it in the house and told my grandfather what happened.

Reread "Piping Plover" and find other verbs that tell about things in the past.

Beside each verb, write the word you would use to tell that the story is happening now.

2. started _____    _____
3. got _____    _____
4. _____    _____
5. _____    _____
6. _____    _____
7. _____    _____

  Write a paragraph about something that happened to you. Underline the verbs that show this story took place in the past.

_____
_____
_____
_____
_____
_____

# Make a 3-D Pet Card

1. Fold two pieces of paper in half.

2. On one page, put a dot near the middle of the folded edge. Draw and cut a 5 cm horizontal line from the dot to the centre of the page.

3. Fold away from the cut to form two triangles.

4. Fold back the triangles. Stand the paper up as in the drawing. Push in the two triangles.

5. Move the mouth by opening and closing the card.

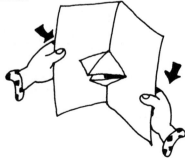

6. Draw a pet around the mouth. Glue the two pages together to make a cover for your card.

Give your finished 3-D pet card to a friend or family member.

# Read and Reflect Grid
## Keeping Old Friends

Use this grid as a guide for reading "Keeping Old Friends."

At each stopping point, jot down notes about what was happening at the time and how the characters were feeling.

| Stopping point | What was happening | How the characters were feeling |
|---|---|---|
| "…'Holly's in the creek!' " (page 72) | | |
| "…we all got wet and stopped laughing." (page 73) | | |
| "…'She's old, but she isn't that sick.' " (page 74) | | |
| " 'Make new friends and keep the old….' " (page 74) | | |
| "…Mom said Holly might die that night." (page 75) | | |
| "…'Holly deserves a few tears.' " (page 75) | | |
| "…for a long, long time." (page 75) | | |

COLLECTIONS 4 Copyright © 1999 Prentice Hall Ginn Canada.
Permission to reproduce this page is restricted to the purchasing school.

KEEPING OLD FRIENDS **17**

# THE ACCIDENT

One May morning
we hear the squeal of brakes.
"Oh no," my mother says;
she knows what the sound means.
Rags lies in the gutter;
she gets up on her front paws
when we run to her
but can't move the back ones.
Mother says, "Her back is broken;
we need to take her to the vet."
We are all crying,
even my Mom and Dad.

The vet says, "She can live
but she'll never walk again."
We talk it over, say goodbye
to Rags, and she licks my hand
through the wire cage
for the last time.
I can't stop crying.

The next day I take
my mother's evening purse
with jewels on the outside,
collect all Rags' hair
from the rug, in the corners
of the room, and under the couch
rub it under my nose, sniff
it, cry some more
and put the purse under some papers
in my desk drawer.

**— DONALD GRAVES**

[Published by B.M.P. from *Baseball, Snakes, and Summer Squash* by
Donald Graves. Copyright © 1966.]

Compare this poem with "Keeping Old Friends." Show
what is the same and what is different in a Venn diagram.

# Contractions

Read each sentence and circle the contractions. Write the two words that form each contraction.

1. Let's see why the dog isn't going in the water.
   _____   _____   _____
   _____   _____   _____

2. Kim said, "I'll bring a ball but I don't have a bat."
   _____   _____   _____
   _____   _____   _____

3. Mom wasn't happy when the new telephone didn't work.
   _____   _____   _____
   _____   _____   _____

Skim "Keeping Old Friends" and find five other contractions. Beside each word write the two little words.

4. _____   _____   _____
5. _____   _____   _____
6. _____   _____   _____
7. _____   _____   _____
8. _____   _____   _____

Find the contractions for these words in the story.

9. was not   _____
10. we had   _____
11. Holly is   _____

12. Look at a piece of writing in which you used contractions. Check the spelling of these words. You might like to add more contractions to your work.

# Suffixes

Read these sentences from "Special Jobs, Special People" and "Rescue K-9-1."

A **suffix** is an ending that is added to a word to make a new word.

Circle words with the suffixes "-ly" and "-ful." Write the root word.

1 My eyes moved (slowly), searching the land ahead for something I could recognize. _slow_____

2 I sat down, completely miserable. _____

3 The trees that had before seemed so beautiful now seemed like looming figures, blocking my view. _____

4 I ran blindly across the swamp and into the hushed woods.

_____

Make new words by adding the suffix "-ly" or "-ful" to the words below. Write a sentence using each new word.

5 friend _____   _____

_____

6 care _____   _____

_____

7 power _____   _____

_____

8 Look at samples of your writing to find words with the suffixes "-ly" and "-ful." Add these to the class chart.

*COLLECTIONS 4* Copyright © 1999 Prentice Hall Ginn Canada.
Permission to reproduce this page is restricted to the purchasing school.

STUDENT WRITING **20**

# Animal Profiles

| eyes | mice |
| --- | --- |
| meadows | foxes |
| geese | cages |
| marshes | hours |
| bushes | butterflies |
| bodies | branches |
|  |  |
|  |  |

eyes
mice
meadows
foxes
geese
cages
marshes
hours
bushes
butterflies
bodies
branches

☐ plurals: -s, -es, and -ies endings; irregular plurals

# Lily Pad Pond

| without | woodland |
| --- | --- |
| remain | toothmarks |
| overnight | bullfrog |
| sunfish | recycle |
| dragonfly | underwater |
| sunbathe | return |
|  |  |
|  |  |

without
woodland
remain
toothmarks
overnight
bullfrog
sunfish
recycle
dragonfly
underwater
sunbathe
return

☐ compound words; words with re- prefix

# The Wounded Wolf

| pause | thawing |
|---|---|
| caused | paws |
| hoof | wolf |
| dawn | hooves |
| crawls | wolves |
| drawing | leaves |
|  |  |
|  |  |

pause
thawing
caused
paws
hoof
wolf
dawn
hooves
crawls
wolves
drawing
leaves

☐ aw and au patterns; plurals: -ves ending

# From a Whale-Watcher's Diary

| noises | oil |
|---|---|
| because | began |
| moist | beneath |
| joins | joy |
| behave | behind |
| voice | pointer |
|  |  |
|  |  |

noises
oil
because
began
moist
beneath
joins
joy
behave
behind
voice
pointer

☐ be- pattern; oi and oy patterns

# Animal Crimes, Animal Clues

| officer | profit |
|---|---|
| photo | wildlife |
| elephants | giraffe |
| microphone | dolphin |
| stuff | found |
| fingerprints | telephone |
|  |  |
|  |  |

Word list:
officer, profit, photo, wildlife, elephants, giraffe, microphone, dolphin, stuff, found, fingerprints, telephone

☐ f, ff, and ph patterns

# The Northern Way

| useful | enough |
|---|---|
| tough | careful |
| toughest | softest |
| biggest | warmest |
| rough | easiest |
| beautiful | laugh |
|  |  |
|  |  |

Word list:
useful, enough, tough, careful, toughest, softest, biggest, warmest, rough, easiest, beautiful, laugh

☐ gh pattern; -ful ending; superlatives

COLLECTIONS 4 Copyright © 1999 Prentice Hall Ginn Canada.
Permission to reproduce this page is restricted to the purchasing school.

# The Puff Adder Who Was Stuck

| orange | gigantic |
|---|---|
| happened | final |
| science | frightened |
| centimetre | endanger |
| enjoy | chicken |
| general | usual |
| | |
| | |

Word list:
- orange
- gigantic
- happened
- final
- science
- frightened
- centimetre
- endanger
- enjoy
- chicken
- general
- usual

☐ soft g pattern; en pattern; -al ending (əl)

# Digging Up Dinosaurs

| horned | carnivore |
|---|---|
| clearly | deer |
| disappear | uncover |
| unwrap | anymore |
| discover | unusual |
| years | dinosaur |
| | |
| | |

Word list:
- horned
- carnivore
- clearly
- deer
- disappear
- uncover
- unwrap
- anymore
- discover
- unusual
- years
- dinosaur

☐ r-controlled patterns: eer, ear, or, er, and aur; un- prefix

# An Interview with Father Goose

| neighbor (neighbour) | eighteen |
| --- | --- |
| thirteen | heavyweight |
| thirty-four | forty-one |
| weight | eighty-two |
| twelve | fifty-eight |
| twenty-one | weigh |

Bookmark:
- neighbor (neighbour)
- eighteen
- thirteen
- heavyweight
- thirty-four
- forty-one
- weight
- eighty-two
- twelve
- fifty-eight
- twenty-one
- weigh

☐ eigh pattern; eight pattern; number words

# You Asked About Pets

| toothbrush | usually |
| --- | --- |
| normally | happily |
| leftovers | easily |
| shelter | computer |
| goldfish | covering |
| overcrowding | probably |

Bookmark:
- toothbrush
- usually
- normally
- happily
- leftovers
- easily
- shelter
- computer
- goldfish
- covering
- overcrowding
- probably

☐ er pattern; -ly ending; compound words

AN INTERVIEW WITH FATHER GOOSE / YOU ASKED ABOUT PETS

# Keeping Old Friends

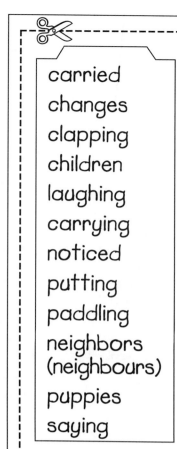

different ending patterns

| carried | changes |
|---|---|
| clapping | children |
| laughing | carrying |
| noticed | putting |
| paddling | neighbors (neighbours) |
| puppies | saying |
|  |  |
|  |  |

# Appendices

# Appendix 1

## Index of Key Learning Expectations/Assessment

| READING | Teaching Opportunities | Assessment Opportunities | | |
|---|---|---|---|---|
| **Overall Expectations** | TRM | TRM | LSC | AH |
| • read a variety of fiction and non-fiction materials for different purposes | pp. 12, 18, 24, 31, 38, 45, 51, 58, 63, 75, 80, 86, 94 | 12, 38, 55, 58, 80 (BLM 17), 84, 94 | 28* | |
| • state their own interpretation of a written work, using evidence from the work and from their own knowledge and experience | pp. 11, 18, 38, 87 | 18 (BLM 4), 22, 38 (BLM 9), 87* | | ⑭, ⑯ |
| **Expectations in Specific Areas** | TRM | TRM | LSC | AH |
| *Reasoning and Critical Thinking*<br>• identify the main idea in a piece of writing, and provide supporting details | pp. 24, 44, 69 | 24*, 44, 49 | | |
| • identify and describe elements of stories | pp. 32, 58, 100, 103 | 32, 100, 103 | | |
| • make inferences while reading | p. 69 | | | |
| • make judgements about what they read on the basis of evidence | | | | ⑭ |
| • retell a story by adapting it for presentation in another way | p. 97 | 97 | | |
| • develop their opinions by reading a variety of materials | p. 80 | 80* (BLM 18) | | |
| • begin to develop research skills | p. 51 | | | |
| *Understanding of Form and Style*<br>• identify various forms of writing and describe their main characteristics | p. 64 | | | ⑯ |
| *Vocabulary Building*<br>• identify synonyms and antonyms for familiar words | p. 75 | 78 | | |

Key:
* Model or Criteria for Checklist/Rubric   ◯ Reading Passages Assessment Master
TRM = Teacher's Resource Module   LSC= Learning Strategy Card   AH = Assessment Handbook

## WRITING

| | Teaching Opportunities | Assessment Opportunities | | |
|---|---|---|---|---|
| **Overall Expectations** | TRM | TRM | LSC | AH |
| • communicate ideas and information for a variety of purposes and to specific audiences | p. 32 | 32 (BLM 7) | | |
| • organize and develop ideas using paragraphs | p. 45 | 49 | 31* | |
| • use simple and compound sentences and vary their sentence structure | p. 25 | 25*, 29 | | |
| • produce pieces of writing using a variety of specific forms and materials from other media to enhance their writing | pp. 13, 19, 52, 59, 64, 70, 76, 88 | 19, 64, 67, 76, 88*, 90 | 29*, 34*, 36*, 38* | |
| • use correctly the conventions (spelling, grammar, punctuation, etc.) specified for this grade level | pp. 81, 91 | 81 (BLM 19), 91 (BLM 20) | | |
| **Expectations in Specific Areas** | TRM | TRM | LSC | AH |
| *Grammar* | | | | |
| • use verb tenses correctly and appropriately | p. 73 | 73 (BLM 15) | | |
| • use connecting words correctly to link ideas in a paragraph | p. 36 | 36 (BLM 8) | | |
| *Word Use and Vocabulary Building* | | | | |
| • choose words that are most effective for their purpose | pp. 39, 56 | 39 (BLM 10), 56 (BLM 14) | | |
| *Visual Presentation* | | | | |
| • label and use pictures and diagrams appropriately | | | | ⑯ |

## ORAL AND VISUAL COMMUNICATION

| | Teaching Opportunities | Assessment Opportunities | | |
|---|---|---|---|---|
| **Overall Expectations** | TRM | TRM | LSC | AH |
| • express and respond to ideas and opinions concisely and clearly | pp. 54, 71 | 54, 71, 72 | 37* | |
| • demonstrate the ability to concentrate by identifying main points and staying on topic | pp. 13, 82 | 13*, 15, 82 | | |
| • analyze media works | pp. 47, 66, 77 | 47* | | |
| **Expectations in Specific Areas** | TRM | TRM | LSC | AH |
| *Non-verbal Communication Skills* | | | | |
| • use appropriate tone of voice and gestures in social and classroom activities | pp. 20, 34 | 35 | | |
| *Media Communication Skills* | | | | |
| • create a variety of media works | pp. 26, 40, 60, 88 | 26, 29, 40, 42, 60*, 61, 88 | 30* | |

*Ontario Edition*

*Appendix 1*    **139**

# Appendix 2 — Teaching Plans at a Glance

| SELECTION | GENRE | LINK TO EXPERIENCE | | READ AND RESPOND TO TEXT | Reading | REVISIT THE TEXT (Mini-Lessons) Writing | Oral Communication |
|---|---|---|---|---|---|---|---|
| Animal Profiles TRM pp. 10–16 | profiles | Think of Ways to Gather Information | Classify Animals | STRATEGY: *Read, Paraphrase, and Teach* / Reader Response | Research an Animal [Assessment] | • Write an Animal Profile • Language Workshop — Spelling | Listen for Fabulous Facts [Assessment] |
| Desert Tortoise TRM pp. 17–22 | poem | Web Desert Information | Read "The Hare and the Tortoise" | STRATEGY: *Listen and Visualize* / Reader Response | Recognize First-Person Voice [Assessment] | Keep a Learning Log [Assessment] | Choral Read the Poem |
| Lily Pad Pond TRM pp. 23–29 | photo essay | Share Knowledge About Ponds | Listen to the Sounds of a Pond | STRATEGY: *Double Look* / Reader Response | Create a Life-Cycle Diagram | • Language Workshop — Style (sentence structure) [Assessment] • Language Workshop — Spelling | |
| The Wounded Wolf TRM pp. 30–35 | picture book story | Recall Information About Wolves | Ask Questions About Wolves | STRATEGY: *Read, Pause, and Reflect* / Reader Response | Diagram the Plot [Assessment] | • Write a Book Cover Synopsis • Language Workshop — Spelling | |
| student writing Animals in the Wild TRM p. 36 | essay factual narrative poem | | | | | • Write an Informational Poem • Language Workshop — Grammar (sentence connectors) | |
| From a Whale-Watcher's Diary TRM pp. 37–42 | diary entries | Display Knowledge About Whales | Discuss Observation Experiences | STRATEGY: *Guided Listen and Read* / Reader Response | Make an Outline [Assessment] | • Language Workshop — Style (word use) • Language Workshop — Spelling | |
| Animal Crimes, Animal Clues TRM pp. 43–49 | article | Tell About Crimes Against Animals | Brainstorm Detective Words | STRATEGY: *Read, Paraphrase, and Teach* / Reader Response [Assessment] | Read Captions | • Write a Paragraph [Assessment] • Language Workshop — Spelling | |
| The Northern Way TRM pp. 50–55 | personal essay | Reflect on Why People Hunt | Recall Information About the Inuit | STRATEGY: *Read and Reflect* / Reader Response | Find Answers in Text [Assessment] | • Write a Group Report • Language Workshop — Spelling | Listen for Details [Assessment] |
| student writing People's Interactions with Wild Animals TRM p. 56 | biography essay book review | | | | | • Write a Book Review • Language Workshop — Usage (temporal markers) | |
| The Puff Adder Who Was Stuck TRM pp. 57–61 | picture book story | Write About Feelings Toward Snakes | Connect with Snake Words | STRATEGY: *Read and Connect* / Reader Response | Find Factual Information [Assessment] | • Write a Sequel • Language Workshop — Spelling | |
| Digging Up Dinosaurs TRM pp. 62–67 | news articles | Draw and Tell About a Dinosaur | Make a Dinosaur Display | STRATEGY: *Narrated Reading* / Reader Response | Analyze the Articles | • Write a Newspaper Article [Assessment] • Language Workshop — Spelling | |
| An Interview with Father Goose TRM pp. 68–72 | interview | Talk About Interviews | Draw a Trained Animal | STRATEGY: *Read and Reflect* / Reader Response | Investigate Vocabulary | • Write a Business Letter • Language Workshop — Spelling | Conduct an Interview [Assessment] |
| student writing People's Interactions with Wild Animals TRM p. 73 | letters memoir | | | | | • Write a Letter • Language Workshop — Grammar (verb tense) | |
| You Asked About Pets TRM pp. 74–78 | questions and answers | Write About Pets | Brainstorm Questions About Pets | STRATEGY: *Double Look* / Reader Response [Assessment] | Identify Synonyms and Antonyms | • Experiment with Typography [Assessment] • Language Workshop — Spelling | |
| Keeping Old Friends TRM pp. 79–84 | short story | Make a Pet Scrapbook | Tell About the Loss of a Pet | STRATEGY: *Read and Reflect* / Reader Response [Assessment] | Compare Ideas in a Story and Poem | • Language Workshop — Style (contractions) • Language Workshop — Spelling | Discuss Pet Problems and Solutions [Assessment] |
| Pet Poems TRM pp. 85–90 | poems | Read Poems About Pets | Make Pet Word Webs | STRATEGY: *Listen and Visualize* / Reader Response | Identify Poetic Techniques | Write a Pet Poem [Assessment] | |
| student writing People and Pets TRM p. 91 | personal narrative poem personal narrative | | | | | • Write a Newspaper Article • Language Workshop — Usage (suffixes) | |

140   *Appendix 2*

| Visual Communication | LINK TO CURRICULUM | | | | LEARNING STRATEGY CARDS | BLACKLINE MASTERS |
|---|---|---|---|---|---|---|
| | *Science*<br>Find Out About Food Chains | *Mathematics*<br>Create and Solve Mathematics Problems | *Language Arts*<br>• Write an Animal Adventure Story<br>• Begin an Animal Word Bank | | #28 Skim and Post-It | BLM 21: Spelling |
| | *Science*<br>Grow a Cactus Garden | *Language Arts*<br>• Read Other Byrd Baylor Books<br>• Develop Word Concepts and Wheels | *Mathematics*<br>Graph Animals' Average Age Expectancies | *The Arts*<br>Create Desert Dioramas | #29 Learning Log | BLM 3: "The Hare and the Tortoise"<br>BLM 4: Who Is Speaking? |
| Diagram Information<br>Assessment | *Language Arts*<br>• Make a Pond Big Book<br>• Generate Lists of Pond Words | *Science*<br>Study Pond Pictures | *The Arts*<br>Paint a Pond Mural | | | BLM 5: Change the Order<br>BLM 21: Spelling |
| Mime the Story<br>Assessment | *Language Arts*<br>Write About Wolf Populations | *Science*<br>Hold a Question/Answer Quiz | *The Arts*<br>Set up a Wolf Display | | | BLM 6: Read, Pause, and Reflect Grid for "The Wounded Wolf"<br>BLM 7: Book Summary for "The Wounded Wolf"<br>BLM 22: Spelling |
| | | | | | | BLM 8: Giving Examples and Reasons |
| Make and Record Observations<br>Assessment | *Language Arts*<br>Read About Tracking Technology | *Mathematics*<br>Record Time Using the 24-hour Clock | *The Arts*<br>• Prepare a Radio Phone Report<br>• Listen to Environmental Music | | #30 Observation Record | BLM 9: Guided Reading Grid for "From a Whale-Watcher's Diary"<br>BLM 10: Word Pictures<br>BLMs 11–12: "Killer Whales Make Cellular Calls!"<br>BLM 22: Spelling |
| Use a Microscope or Magnifying Glass | *Language Arts*<br>Make Animal Crime Cards | *Science*<br>Research Crime-Solving Instruments | *The Arts*<br>Compose a Song | | #31 Writing a Paragraph | BLM 23: Spelling |
| | *The Arts*<br>Make an Animal Print | *Science*<br>Write an Animal Profile | *Language Arts*<br>• Create a Glossary<br>• Read About the Inuit | | #32 Report | BLM 13: "Musk Oxen"<br>BLM 23: Spelling |
| | | | | | #33 Book Review | BLM 14: Words That Show Time |
| Look at and Draw Borders<br>Assessment | *Language Arts*<br>Expand Vocabulary | *Science*<br>Research Snakes | *The Arts*<br>Pantomime a Scene | | | BLM 24: Spelling |
| Look Closely at a Picture | *Language Arts*<br>Define Paleontology Words | *Social Studies*<br>Locate Dinosaur Sites | *Science*<br>Investigate Dinosaur Extinction | *The Arts*<br>Make a Fossil | #34 Newspaper Article<br>#35 Using the Internet | BLM 24: Spelling |
| | *Language Arts*<br>Prepare Interview Questions | *Science*<br>Investigate Migration | *The Arts*<br>Design a Poster | | #36 Business Letter<br>#37 Interviewing | BLM 25: Spelling |
| | | | | | | BLM 15: Verbs in the Past |
| View Animals in Art | *Language Arts*<br>Read Stories About Pets | *Science*<br>Research Pets | *The Arts*<br>Make a 3-D Pet Card | | | BLM 16: Make a 3-D Pet Card<br>BLM 25: Spelling |
| | *Language Arts*<br>Draw a Cartoon Strip | *Science*<br>Research Dogs | *The Arts*<br>• Role-Play Consoling a Friend<br>• Make a Line Drawing | | | BLM 17: Read and Reflect Grid for "Keeping Old Friends"<br>BLM 18: "The Accident"<br>BLM 19: Contractions<br>BLM 26: Spelling |
| Represent Ideas Visually<br>Assessment | *Language Arts*<br>Find Out About a Poet | *The Arts*<br>• Choose Music for a Poem<br>• Make a Pet Poetry Book | *Mathematics*<br>Conduct a Survey | | #38 Concrete and Shape Poetry | |
| | | | | | | BLM 20: Suffixes |

*Appendix 2*   141

# Appendix 3    Unit Spelling Words

### ANIMAL PROFILES
- *plurals: -s, -es, and -ies endings; irregular plurals*

| eyes | mice |
| meadows | foxes |
| geese | cages |
| marshes | hours |
| bushes | butterflies |
| bodies | branches |

**Theme/Challenge Words**
- *animal words*

hibernate     species
chrysalis     caterpillars
fierceness

**Early Words**
- *wh pattern; sh pattern*

white    whale    when
fish     ship

### LILY PAD POND
- *compound words; words with re- prefix*

without      woodland
remain       toothmarks
overnight    bullfrog
sunfish      recycle
dragonfly    underwater
sunbathe     return

**Theme/Challenge Words**
- *animal words*

breathe         nymph
reproduction    creature
reproduce

**Early Words**
- *consonant blends*

dry      fly      plant
stand    want

### THE WOUNDED WOLF
- *aw and au patterns; plurals: -ves ending*

pause     thawing    caused
paws      hoof       wolf
dawn      hooves     crawls
wolves    drawing    leaves

**Theme/Challenge Words**
- *adventure words*

procession    celebration
gnashes       deathwatch
ghostly

**Early Words**
- *ck pattern*

pack    peck    picks
rock    back

### FROM A WHALE-WATCHER'S DIARY
- *be- pattern; oi and oy patterns*

noises    oil      because
began     moist    beneath
joins     joy      behave
behind    voice    pointer

**Theme/Challenge Words**
- *whale study words*

identification    echolocation
acoustic          hydrophone
research

**Early Words**
- *long e patterns: ee and ea*

sleep    seem    hear
each     lead

### ANIMAL CRIMES, ANIMAL CLUES
- *f, ff, and ph patterns*

officer         profit
photo           wildlife
elephants       giraffe
microphone      dolphin
stuff           found
fingerprints    telephone

**Theme/Challenge Words**
- *crime solution words*

microscope    detective
forensics     laboratory
photographer

**Early Words**
- *consonant digraphs and blends*

snake    crime    while
shape    stripe

### THE NORTHERN WAY
- *gh pattern; -ful ending; superlatives*

useful      enough
tough       careful
toughest    softest
biggest     warmest
rough       easiest
beautiful   laugh

**Theme/Challenge Words**
- *northern words*

Inuit         caribou
snowmobiles   permafrost
ptarmigan

**Early Words**
- *z patterns*

froze    zero    prize
these    use

### THE PUFF ADDER WHO WAS STUCK
- *soft g pattern; en pattern; -l ending (əl)*

orange       gigantic
happened     final
science      frightened
centimetre   endanger
enjoy        chicken
general      usual

**Theme/Challenge Words**
- *feeling words*

petrified    nervous
commotion    excitement
frantically

**Early Words**
- *double ending consonants*

off     mitt     yell
hiss    still

### DIGGING UP DINOSAURS
- *r-controlled patterns: eer, ear, or, er, and aur; un- prefix*

horned       carnivore
clearly      deer
disappear    uncover
unwrap       anymore
discover     unusual
years        dinosaur

**Theme/Challenge Words**
- *dinosaur words*

prehistoric    skeletons
museum         fossilized
Tyrannosaurus rex

**Early Words**
- *sounds of oo pattern*

tools    tooth    hoop
hook     took

### AN INTERVIEW WITH FATHER GOOSE
- *eigh pattern; eight pattern; number words*

neighbor (-our)    eighteen
thirteen           heavyweight
thirty-four        forty-one
weight             eighty-two
twelve             fifty-eight
twenty-one         weigh

**Theme/Challenge Words**
- *occupation words*

scientist    paleontologist
biologist    naturalist    zoologist

**Early Words**
- *high utility words*

walks    who    two
very     think

### YOU ASKED ABOUT PETS
- *er pattern; -ly ending; compound words*

toothbrush      usually
normally        happily
leftovers       easily
shelter         computer
goldfish        covering
overcrowding    probably

**Theme/Challenge Words**
- *pet words*

veterinarian      gene    aquarium
behavior (-our)   gerbils

**Early Words**
- *oo and ou patterns*

could    would    should
good     look

### KEEPING OLD FRIENDS
- *different ending patterns*

carried     changes
clapping    children
laughing    carrying
noticed     putting
paddling    neighbors (-ours)
puppies     saying

**Theme/Challenge Words**
- *dog words*

retriever    Airedale
students' choices of other breeds of dogs

**Early Words**
- *-ed ending*

walked    helped    jumped
sailed    rolled

142   *Appendix 3*